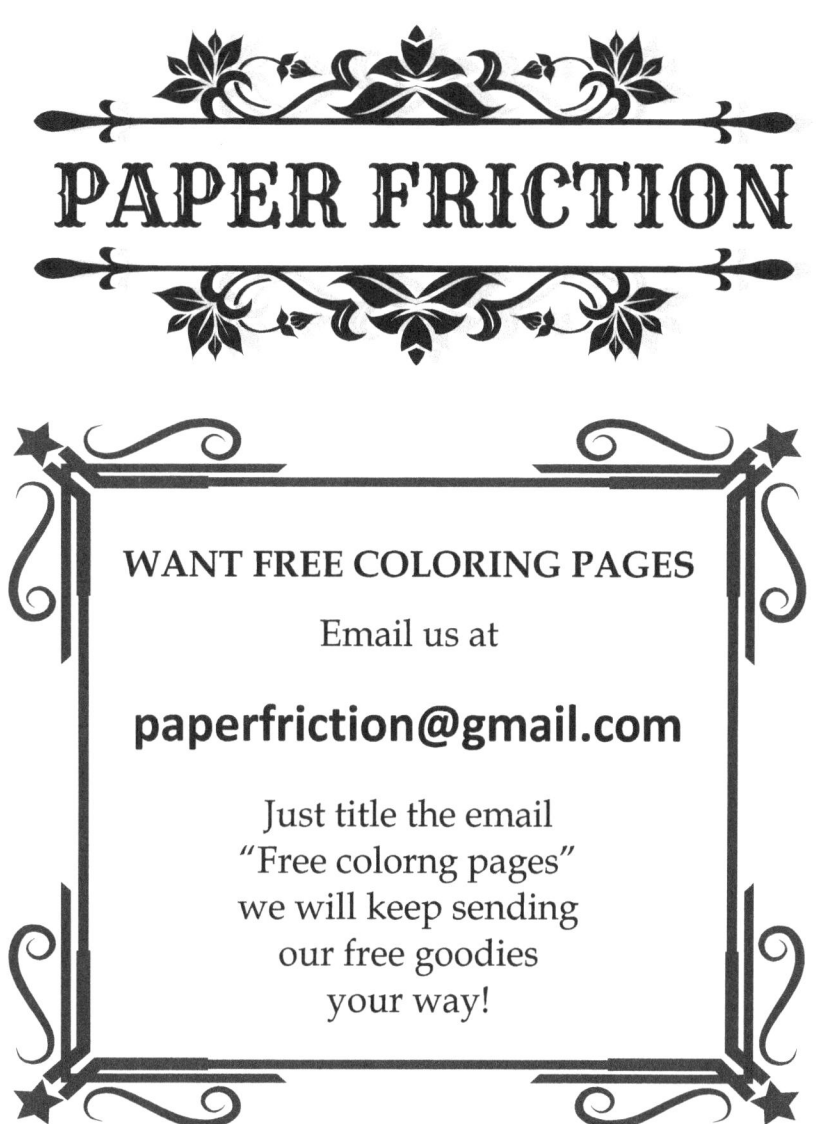

PAPER FRICTION

WANT FREE COLORING PAGES

Email us at

paperfriction@gmail.com

Just title the email
"Free colorng pages"
we will keep sending
our free goodies
your way!

We value our customers and always welcome feedback and suggestions.
If you would like to connect with us please e-mail **paperfriction@gmail.com**
and we will get back to you as soon as possible.

Join our facebook group community for our Contest and Updates.
www.facebook.com/groups/paperfriction/

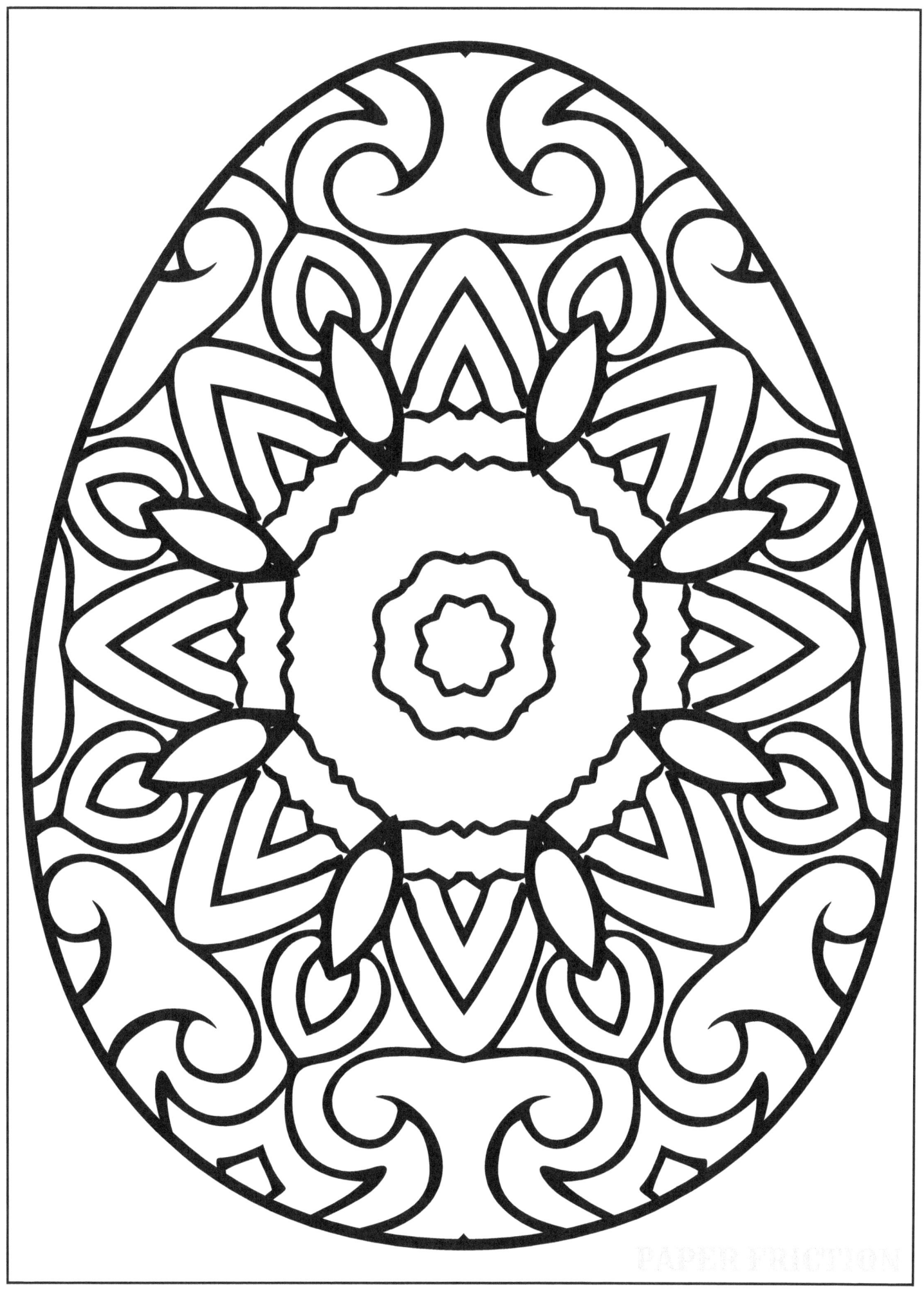

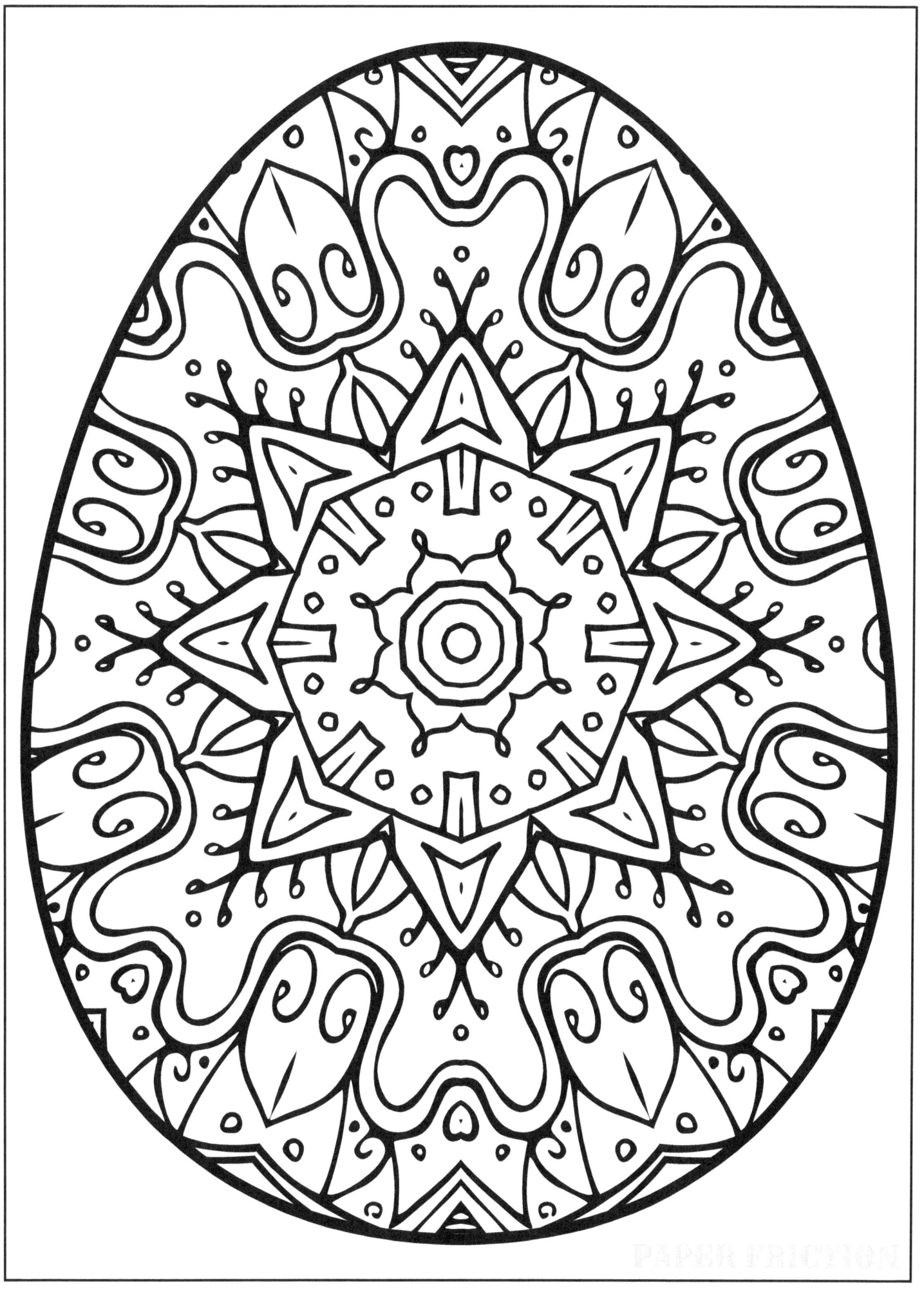

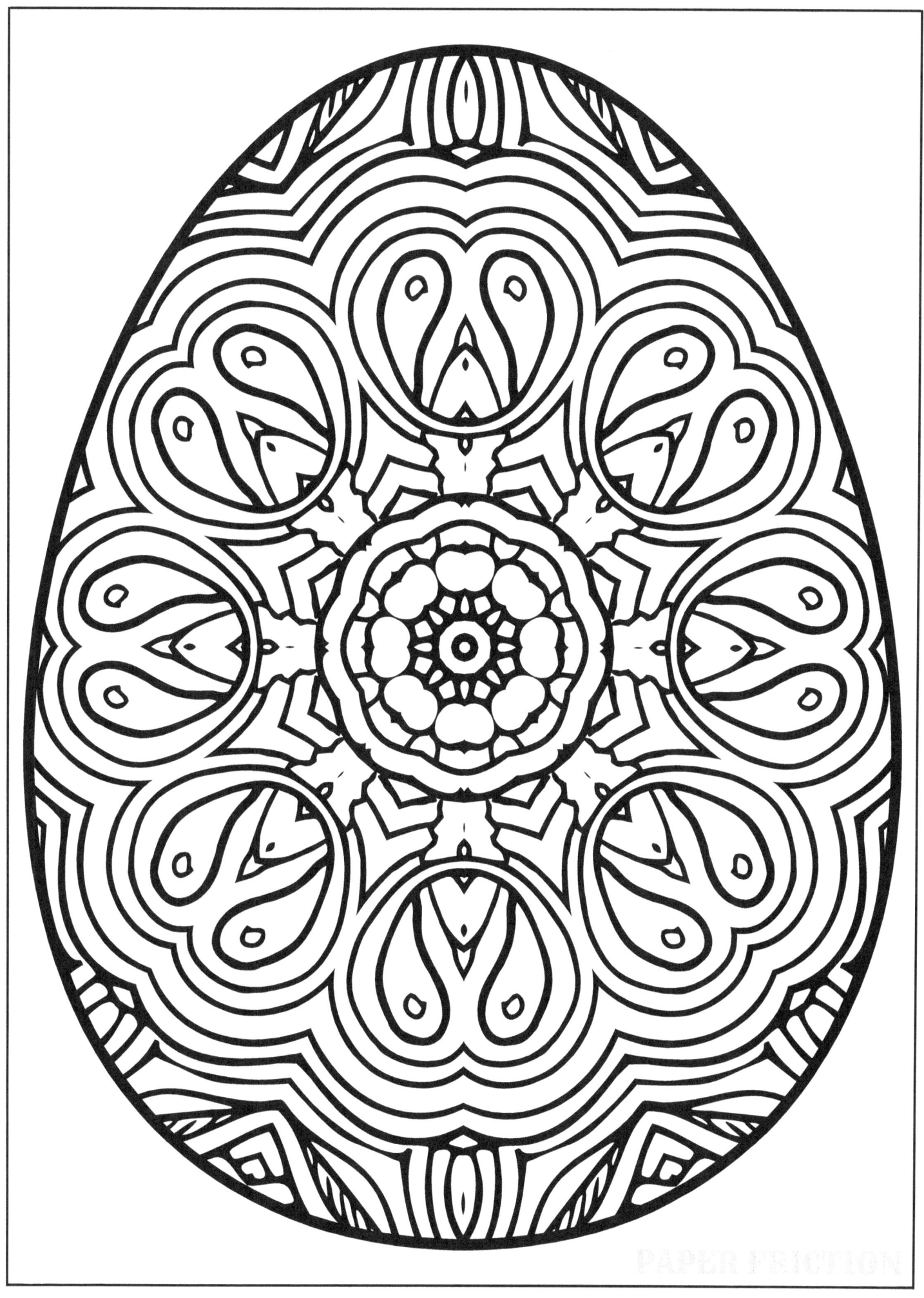

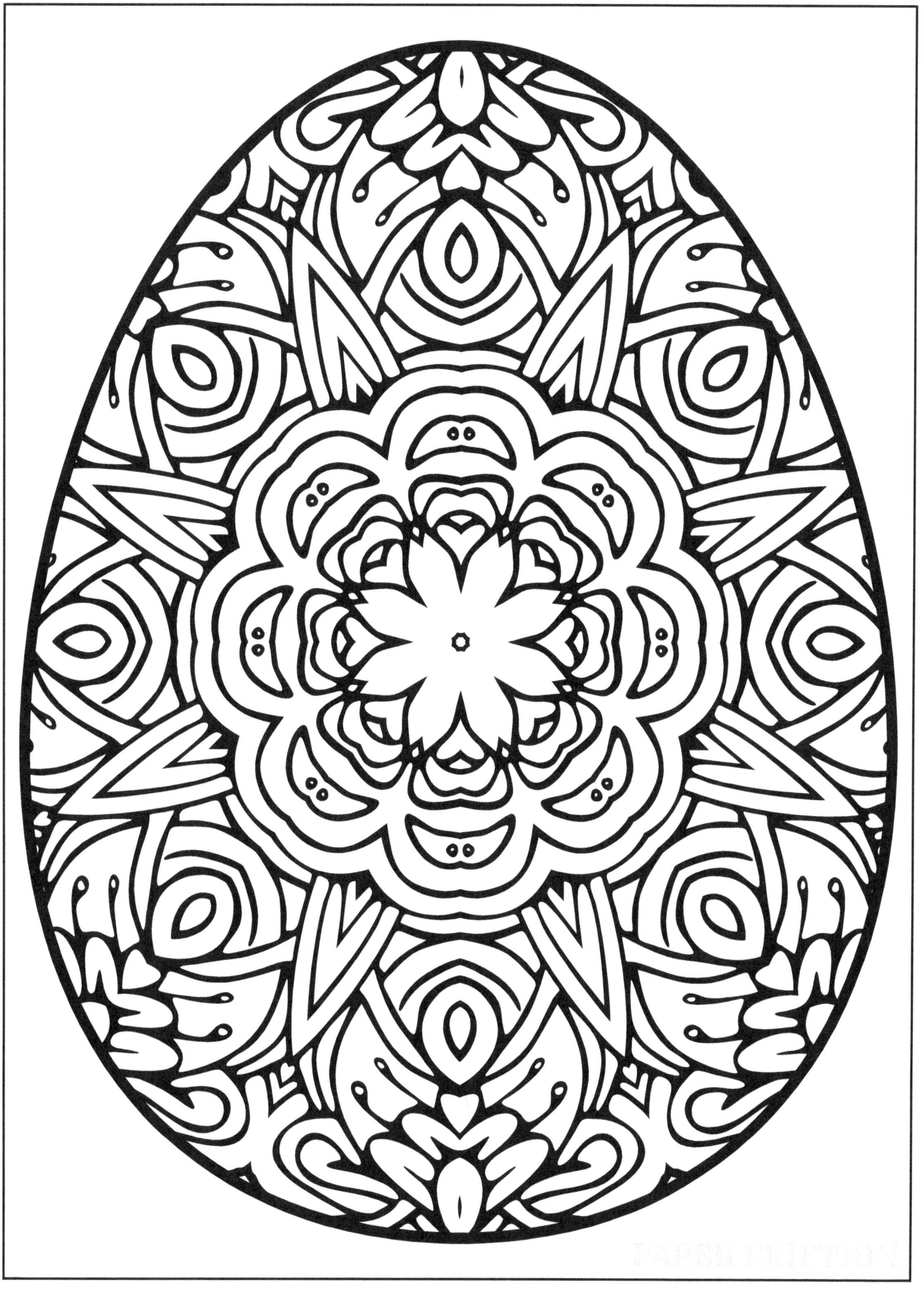

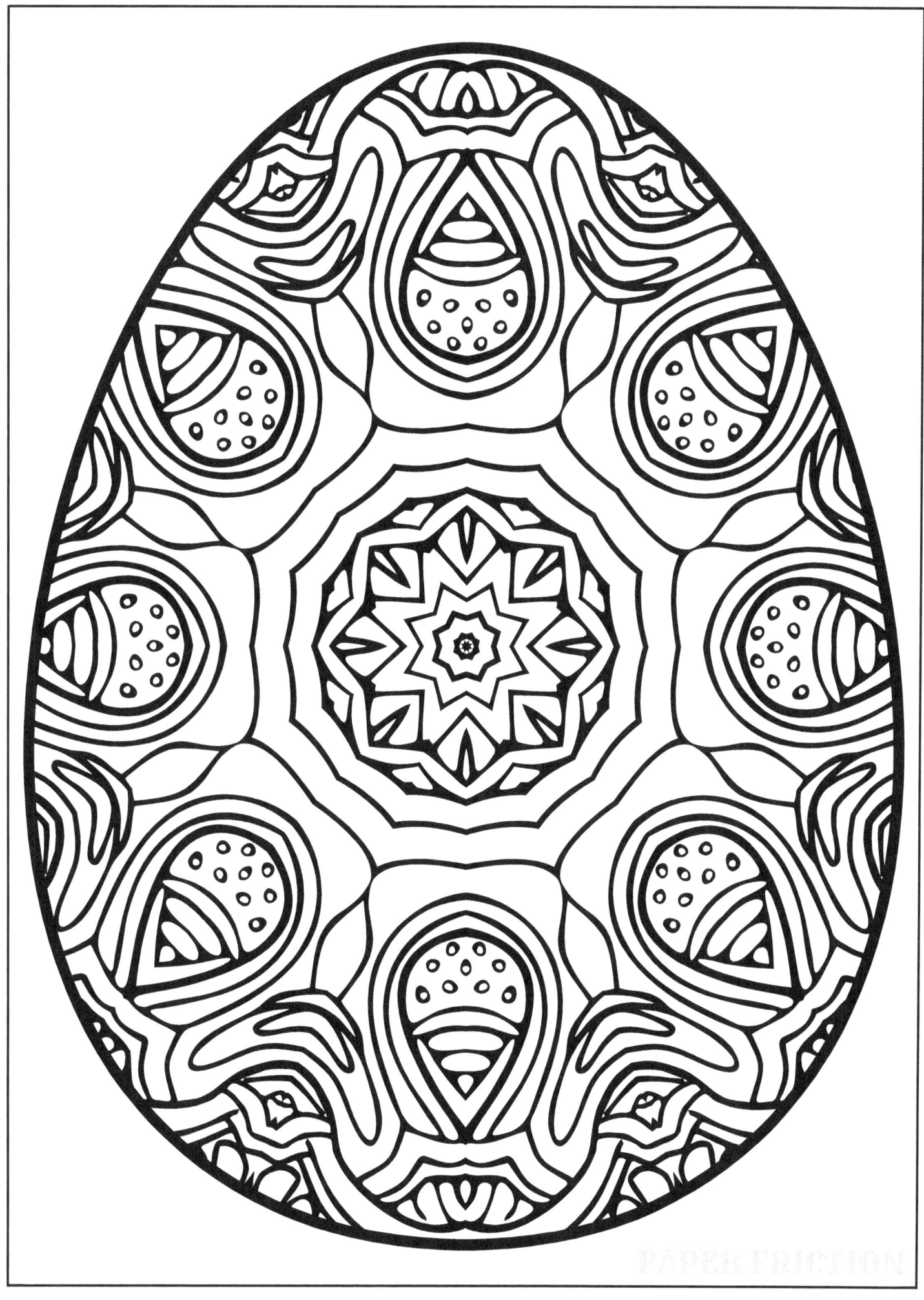

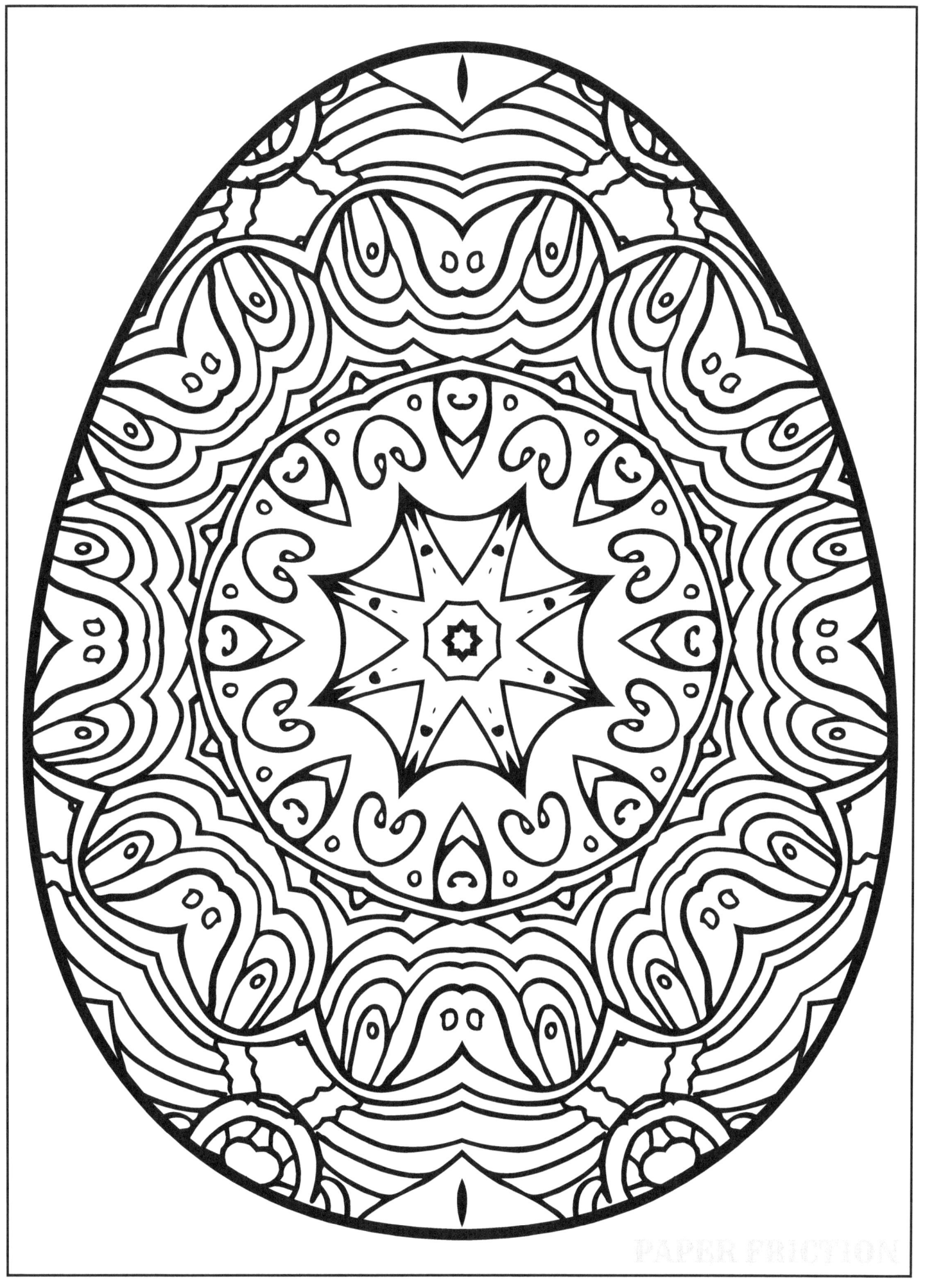

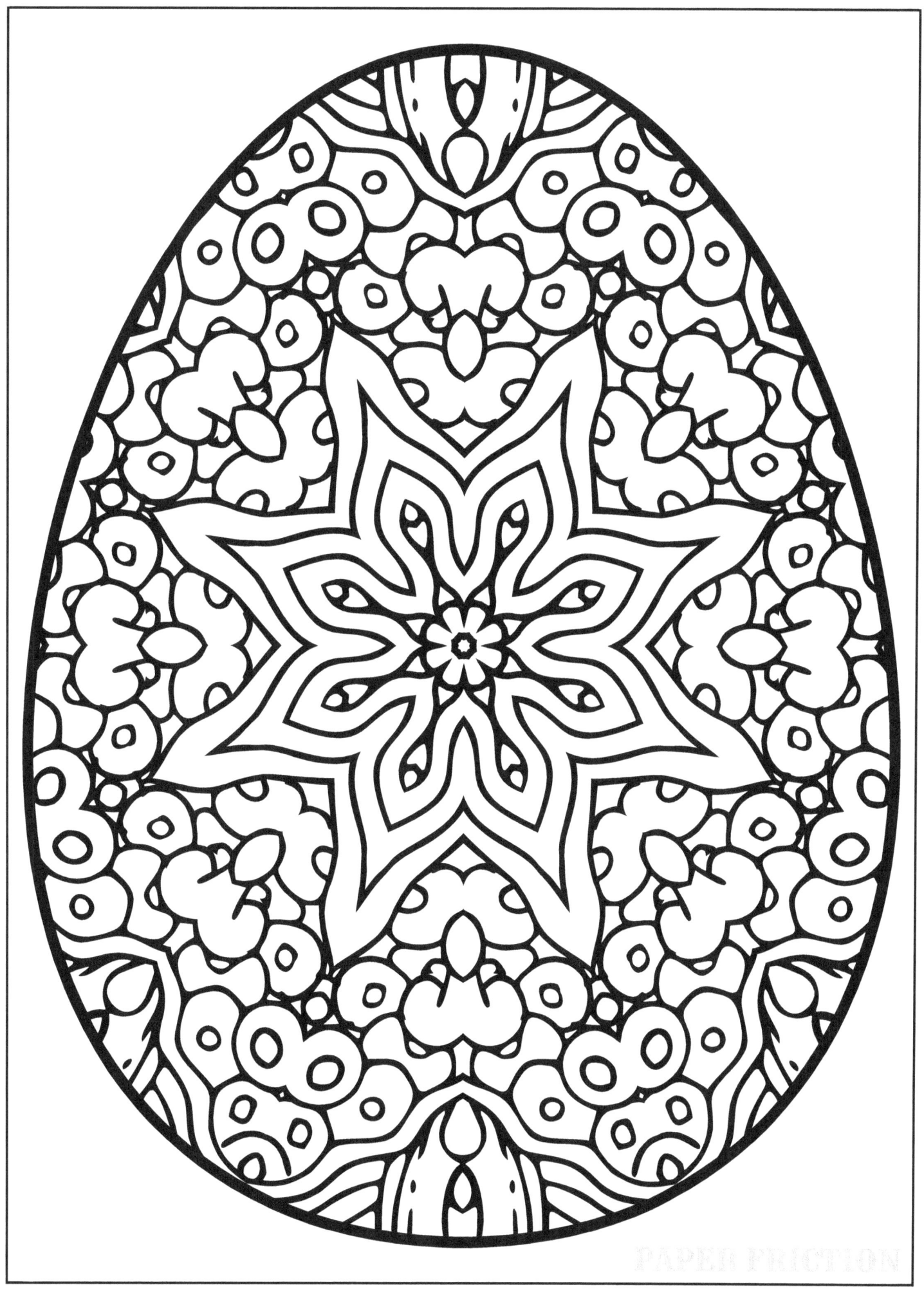

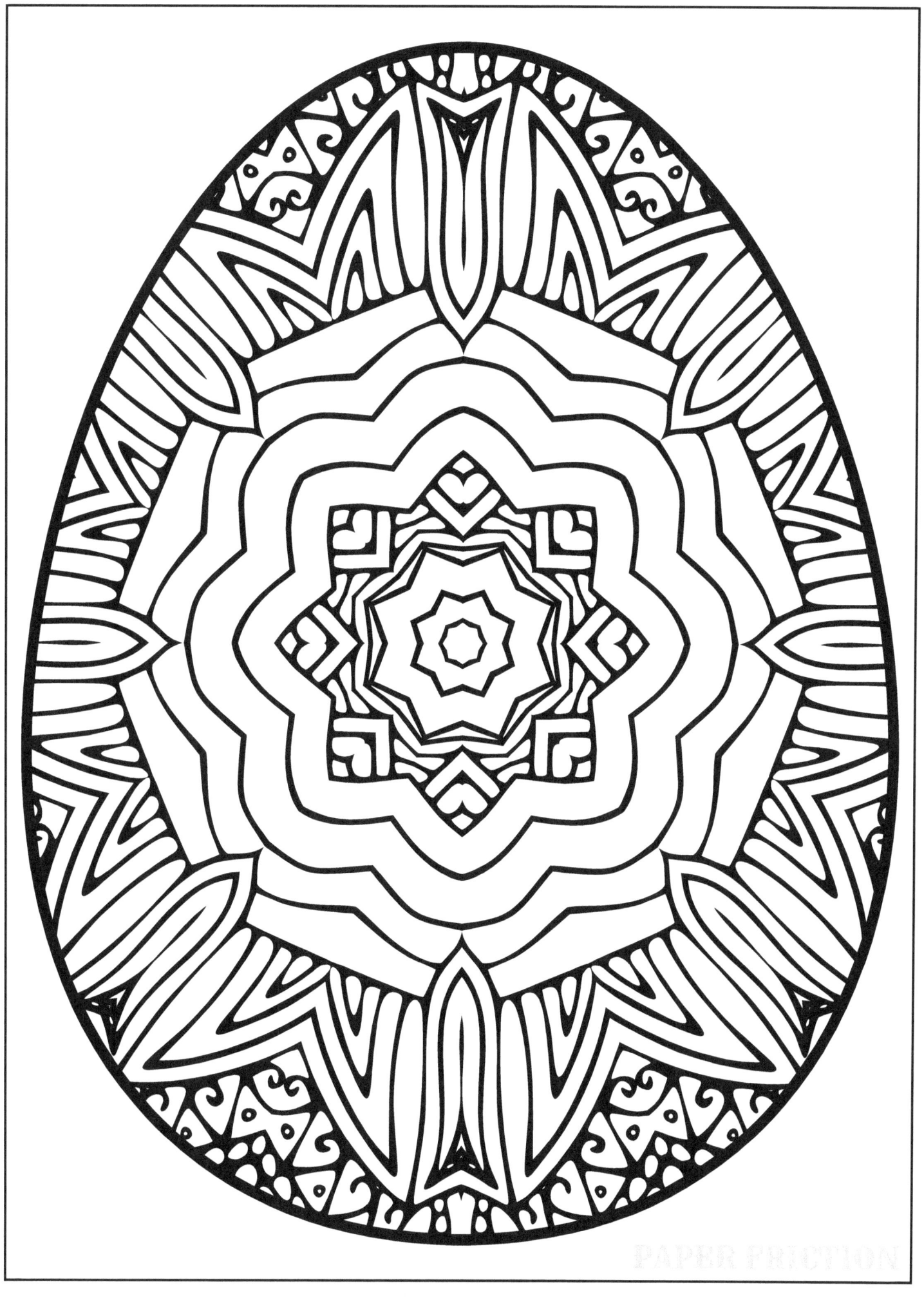

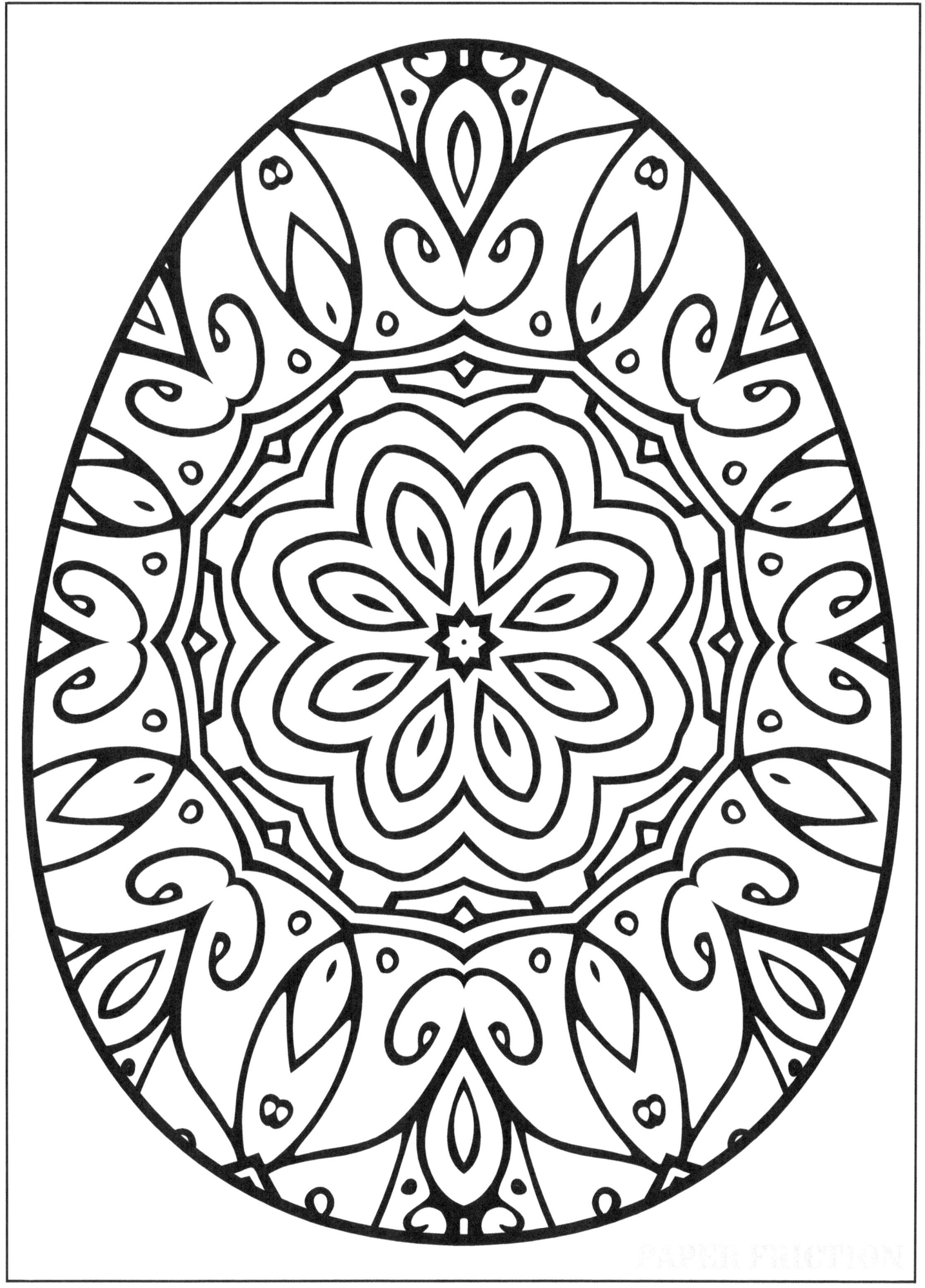

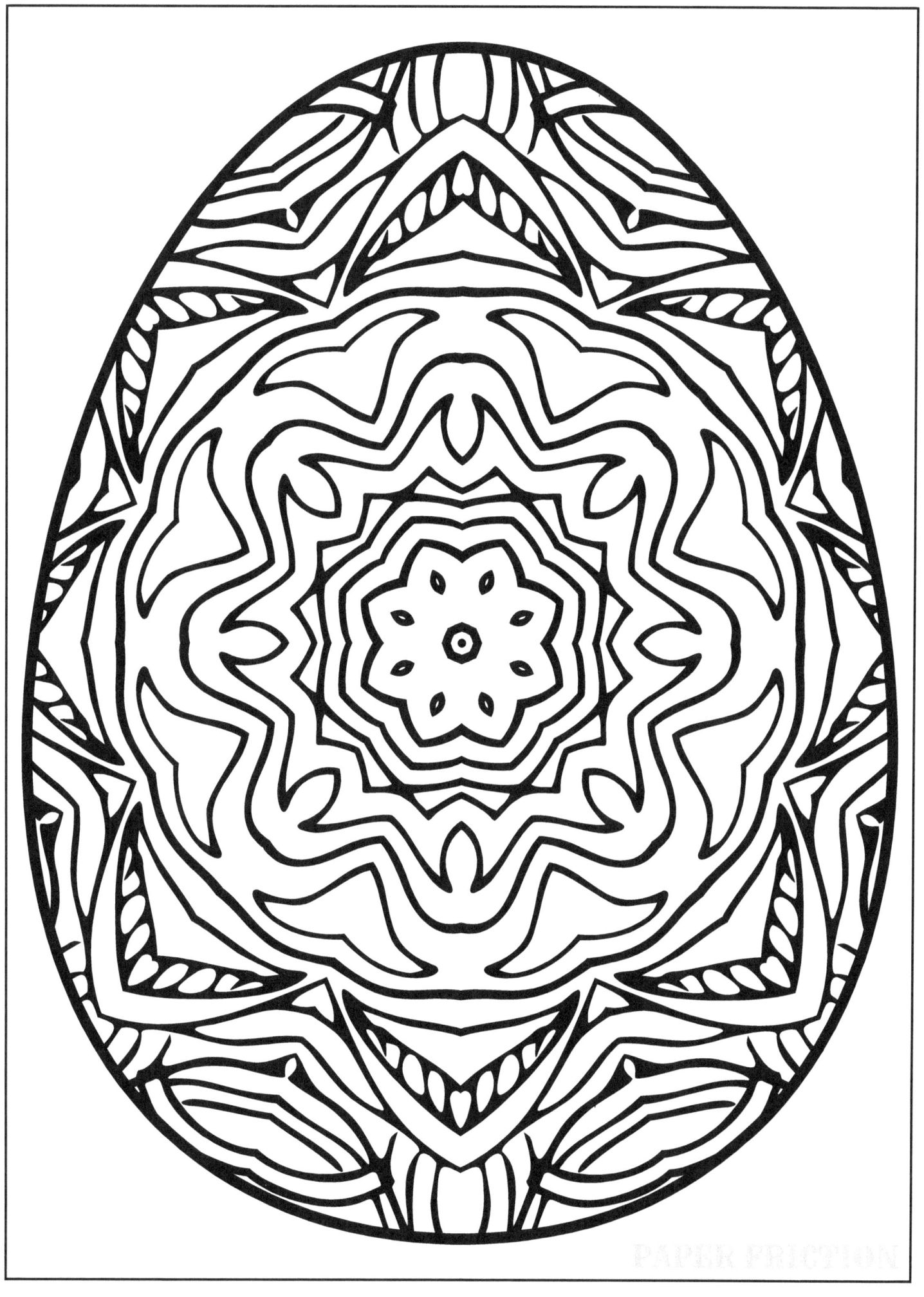

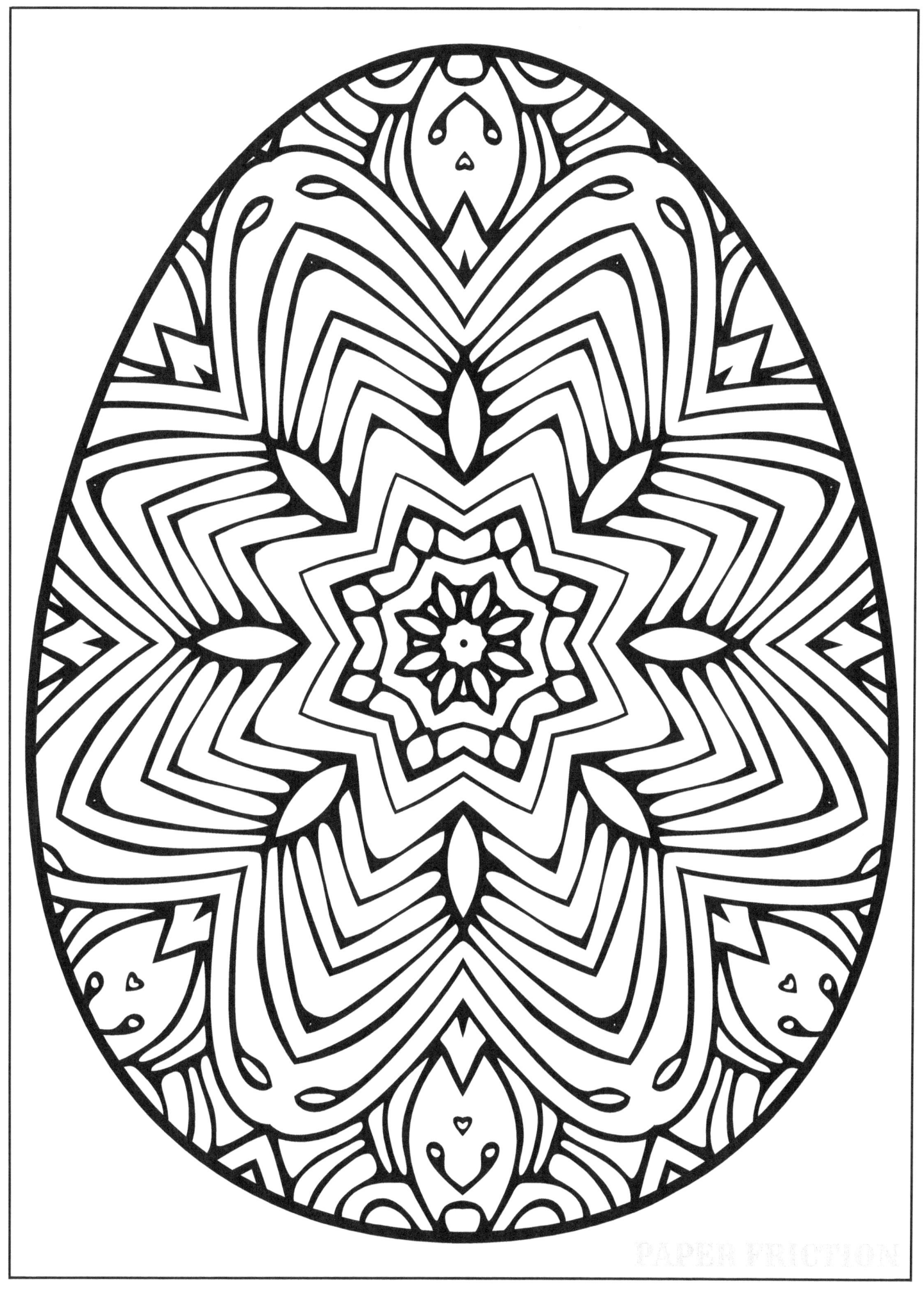

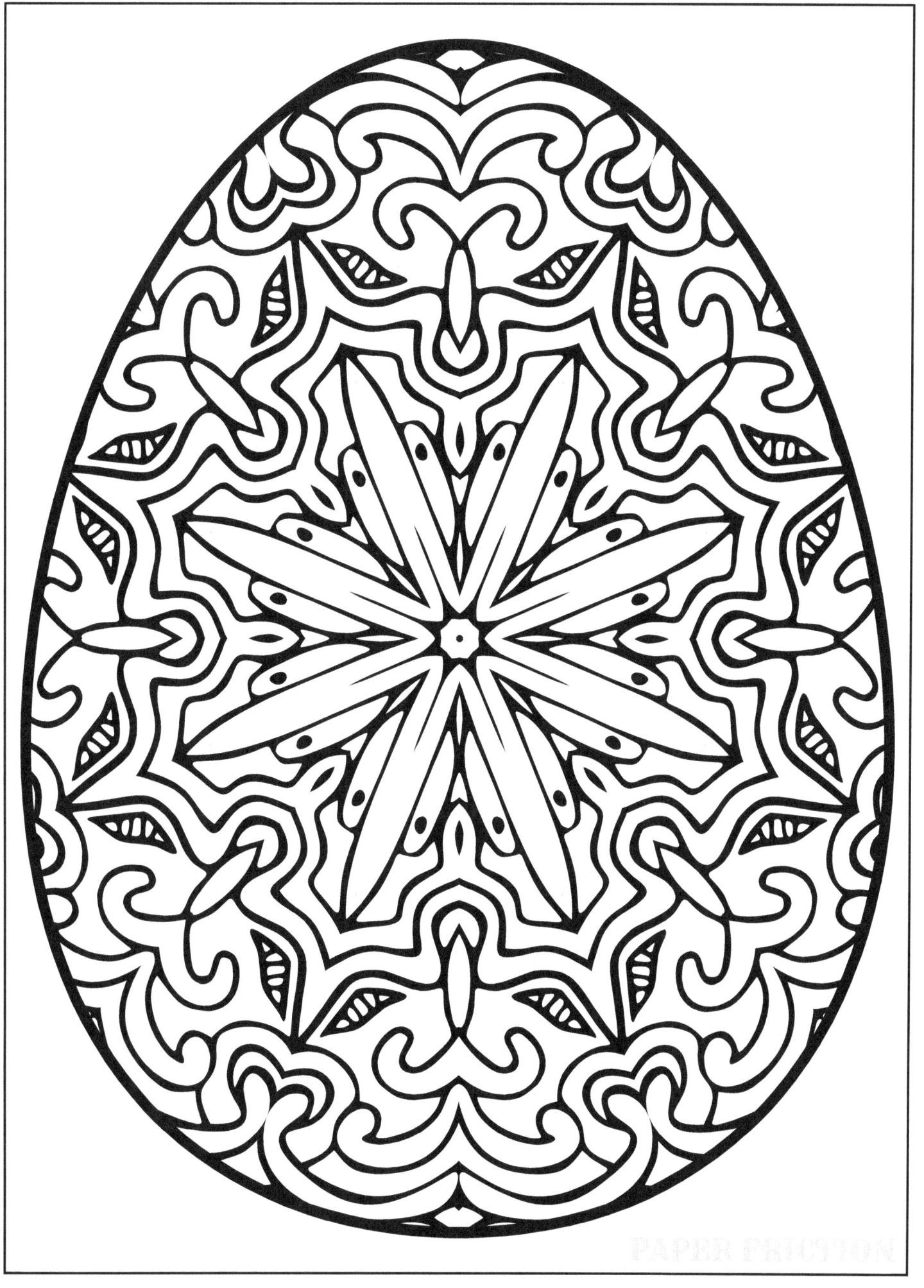

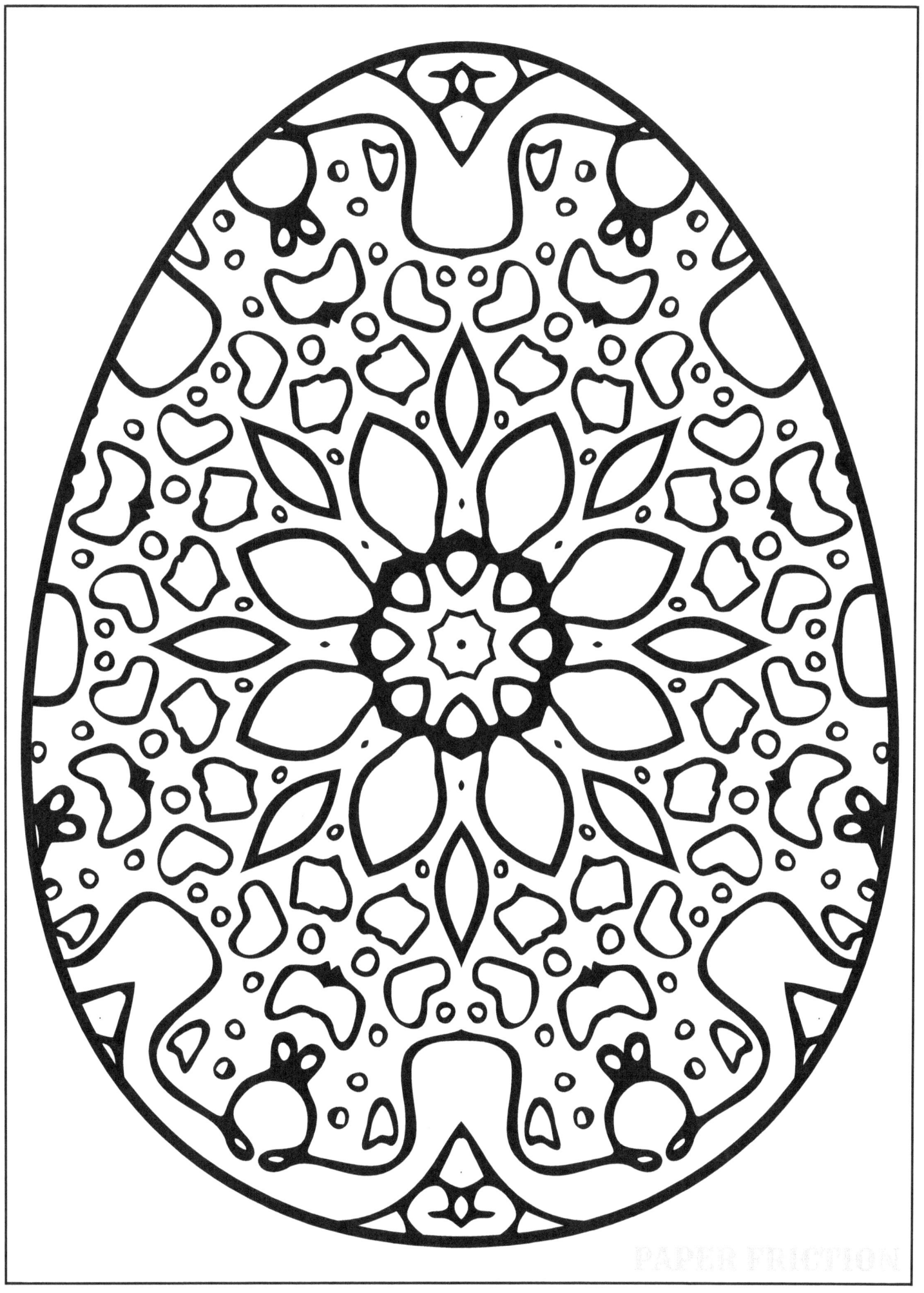

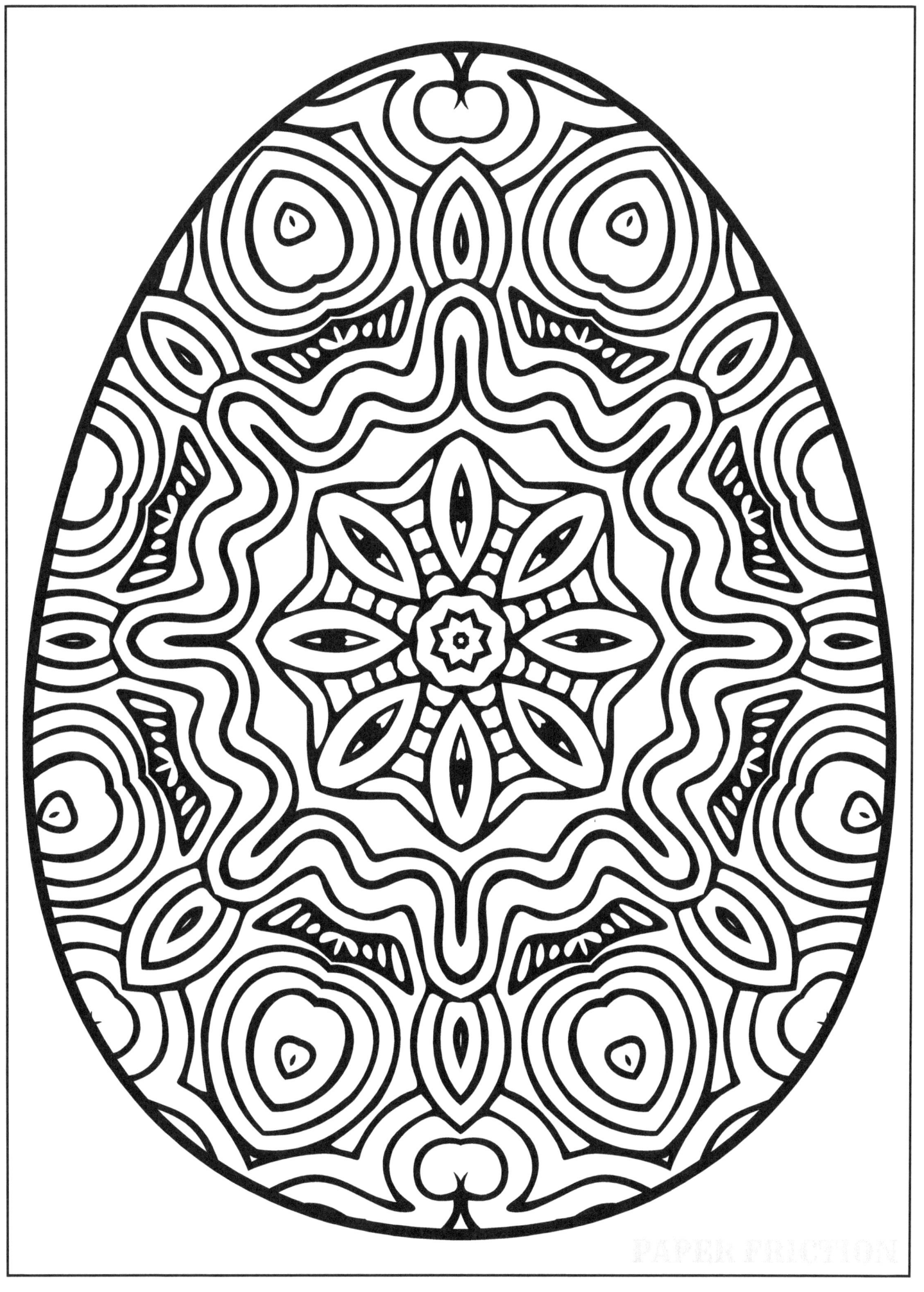

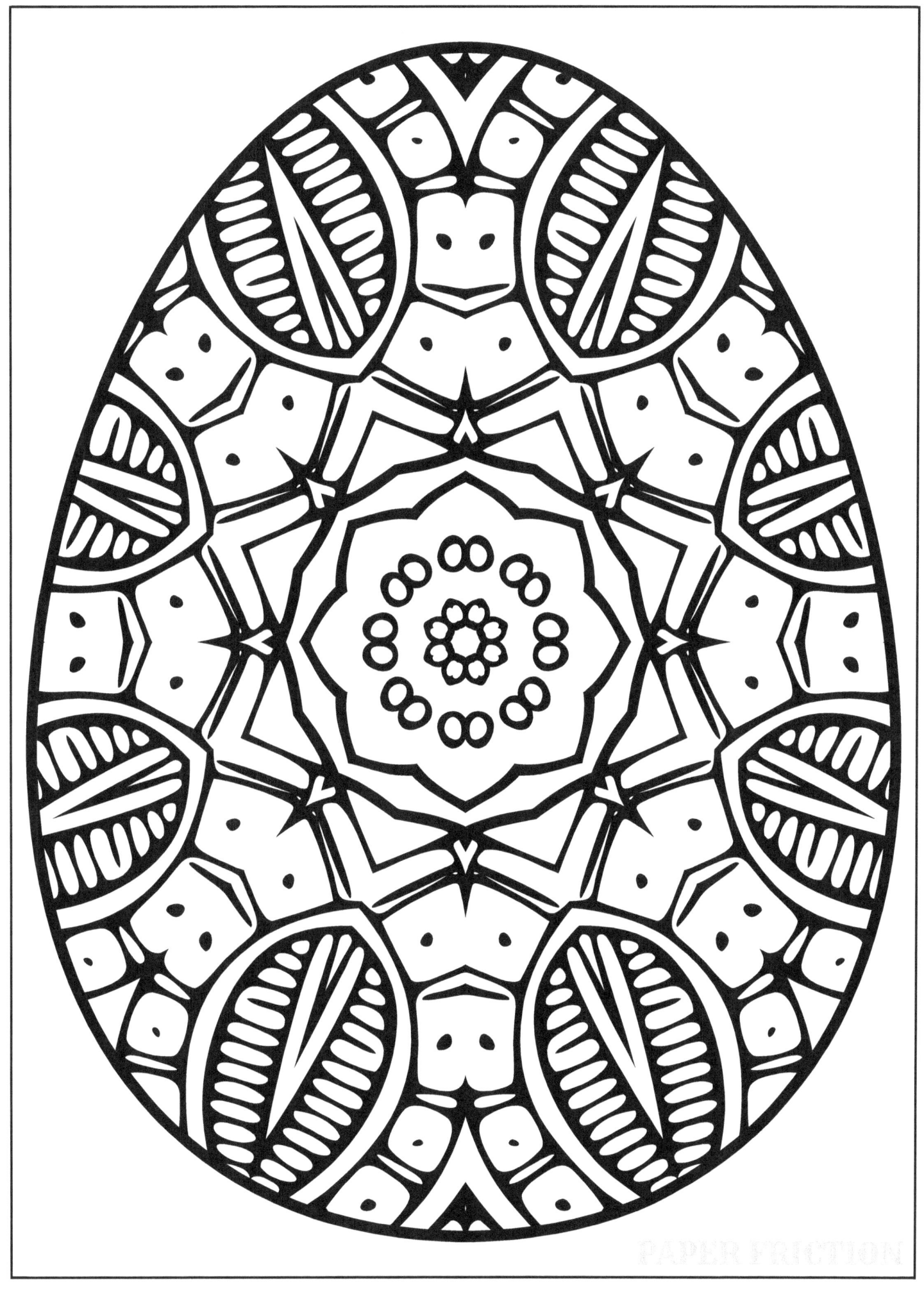

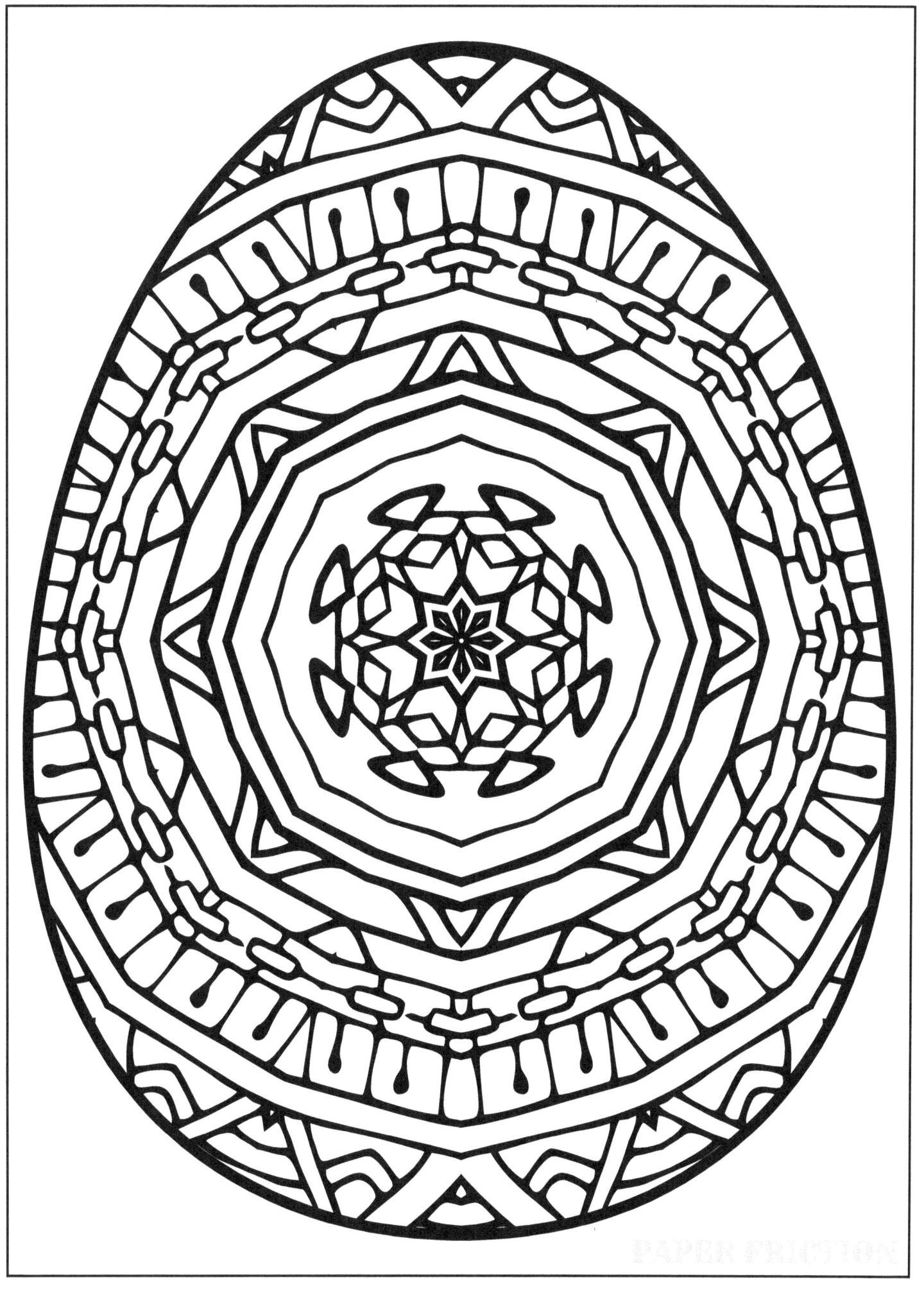

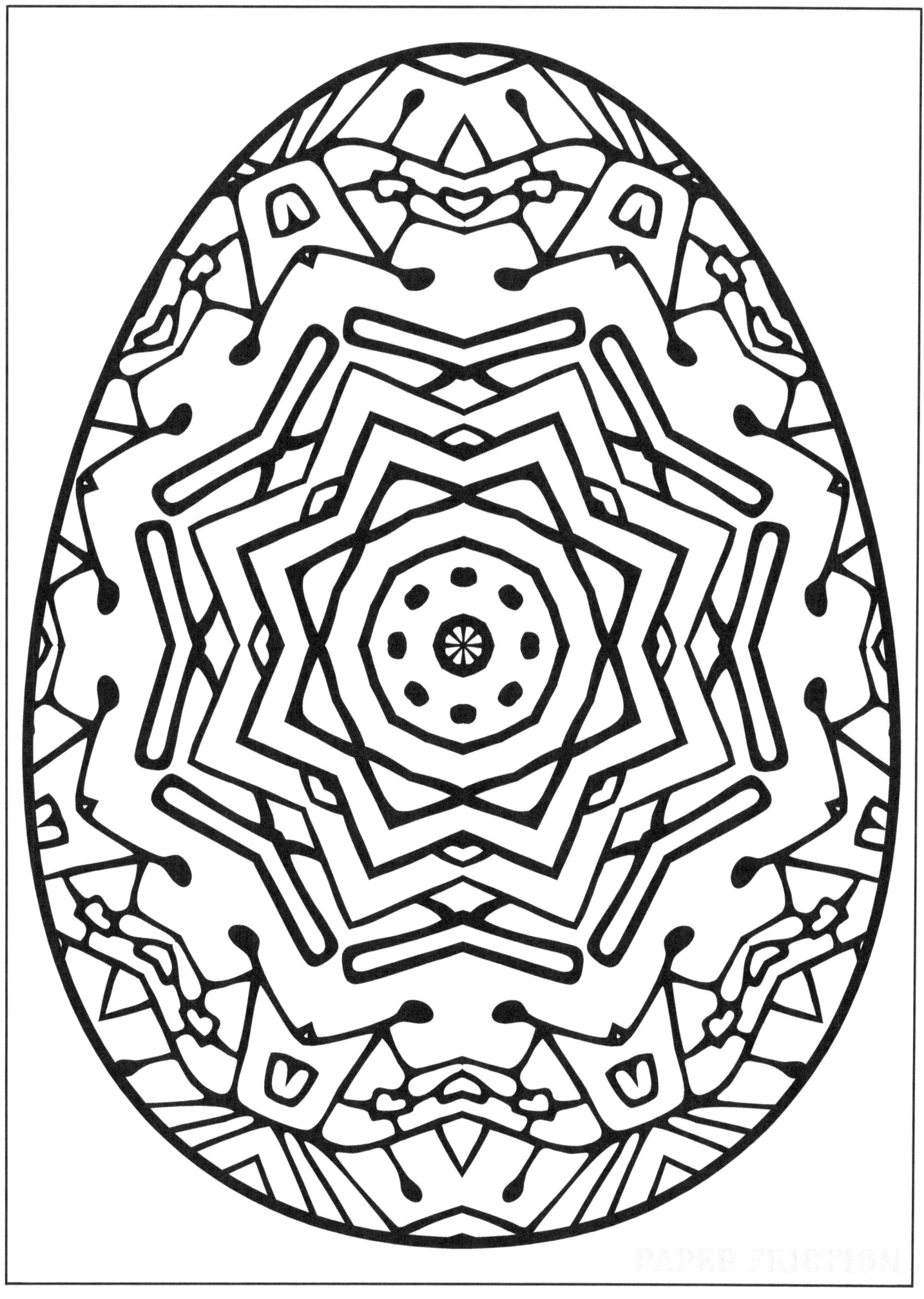

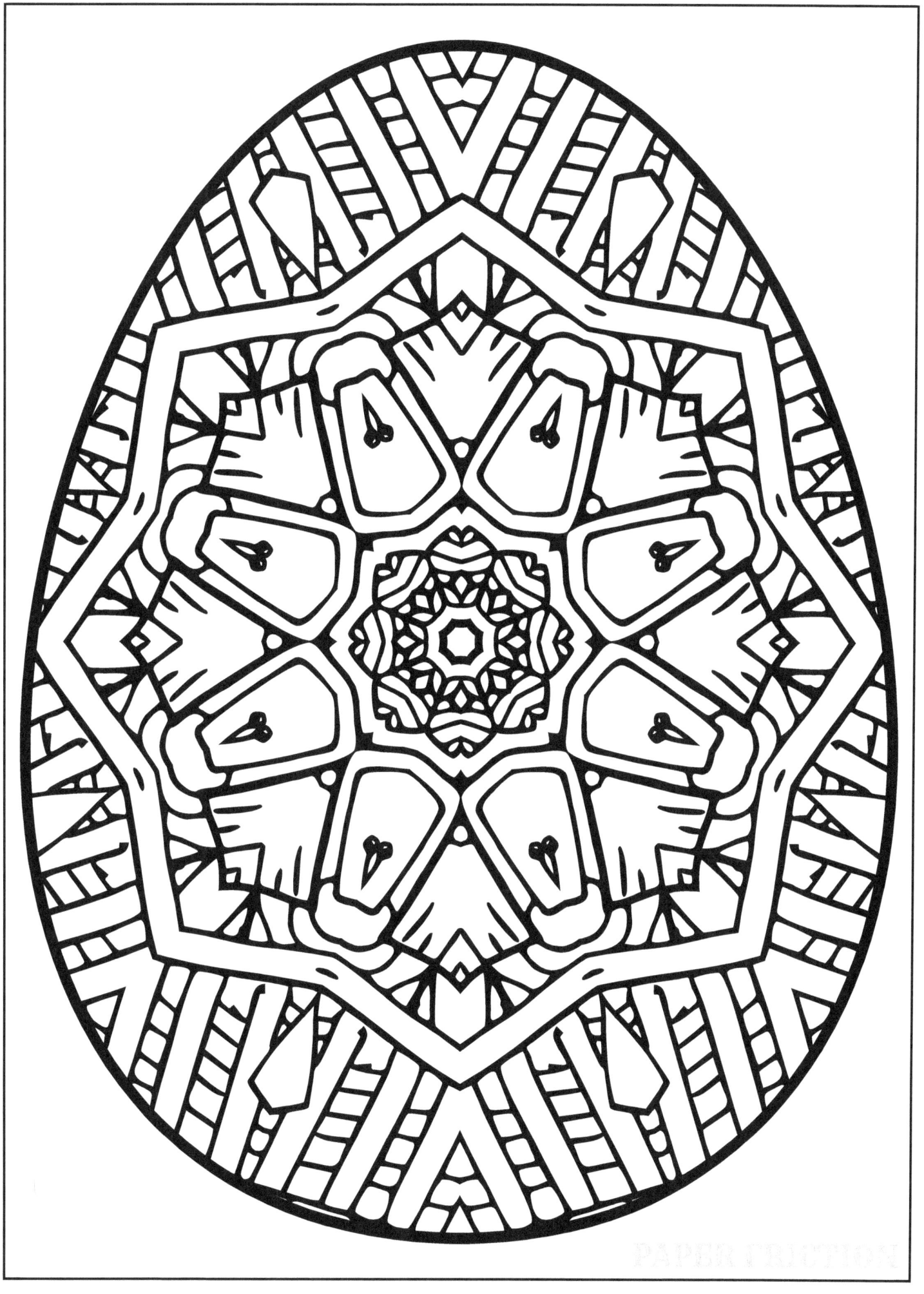

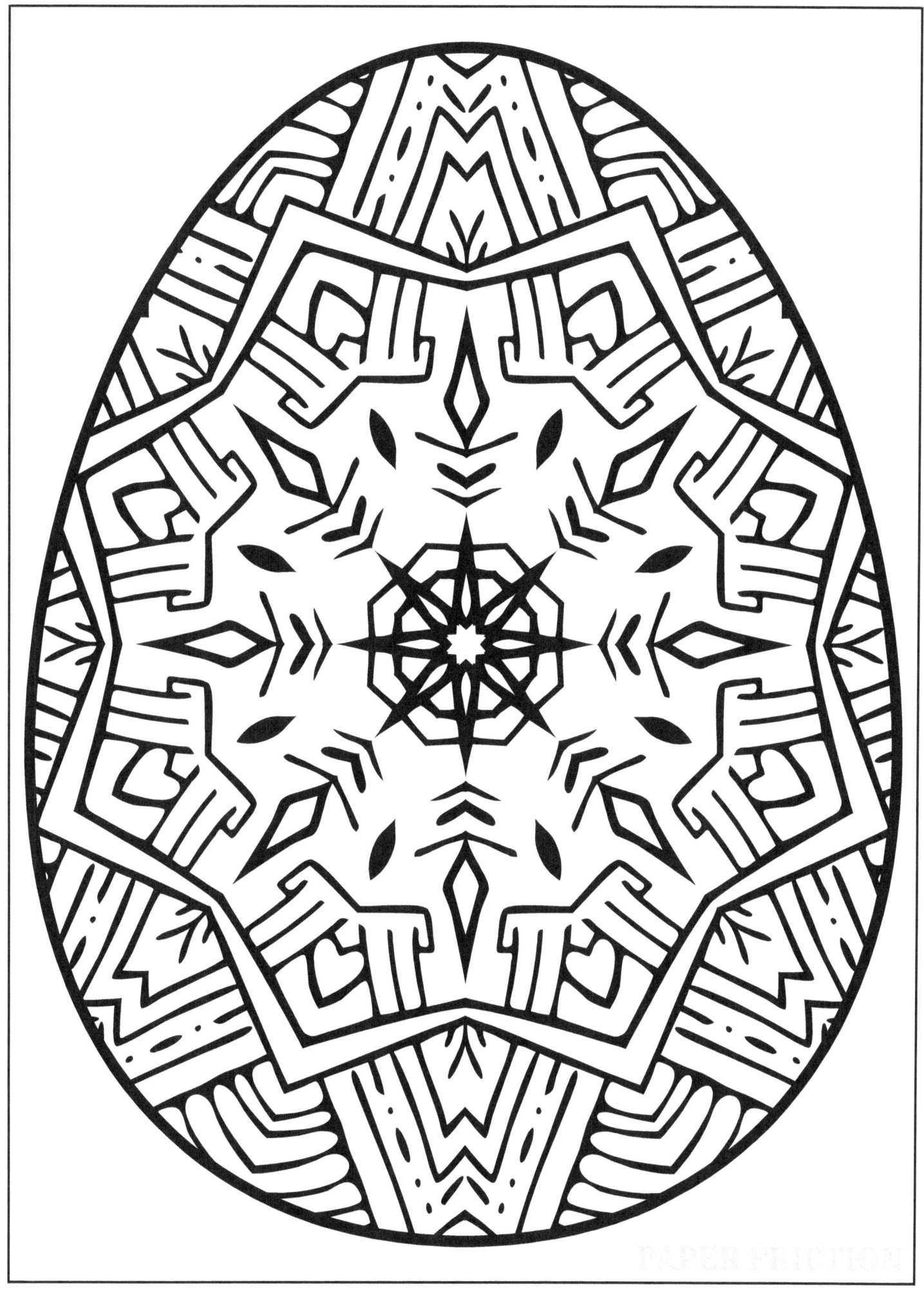

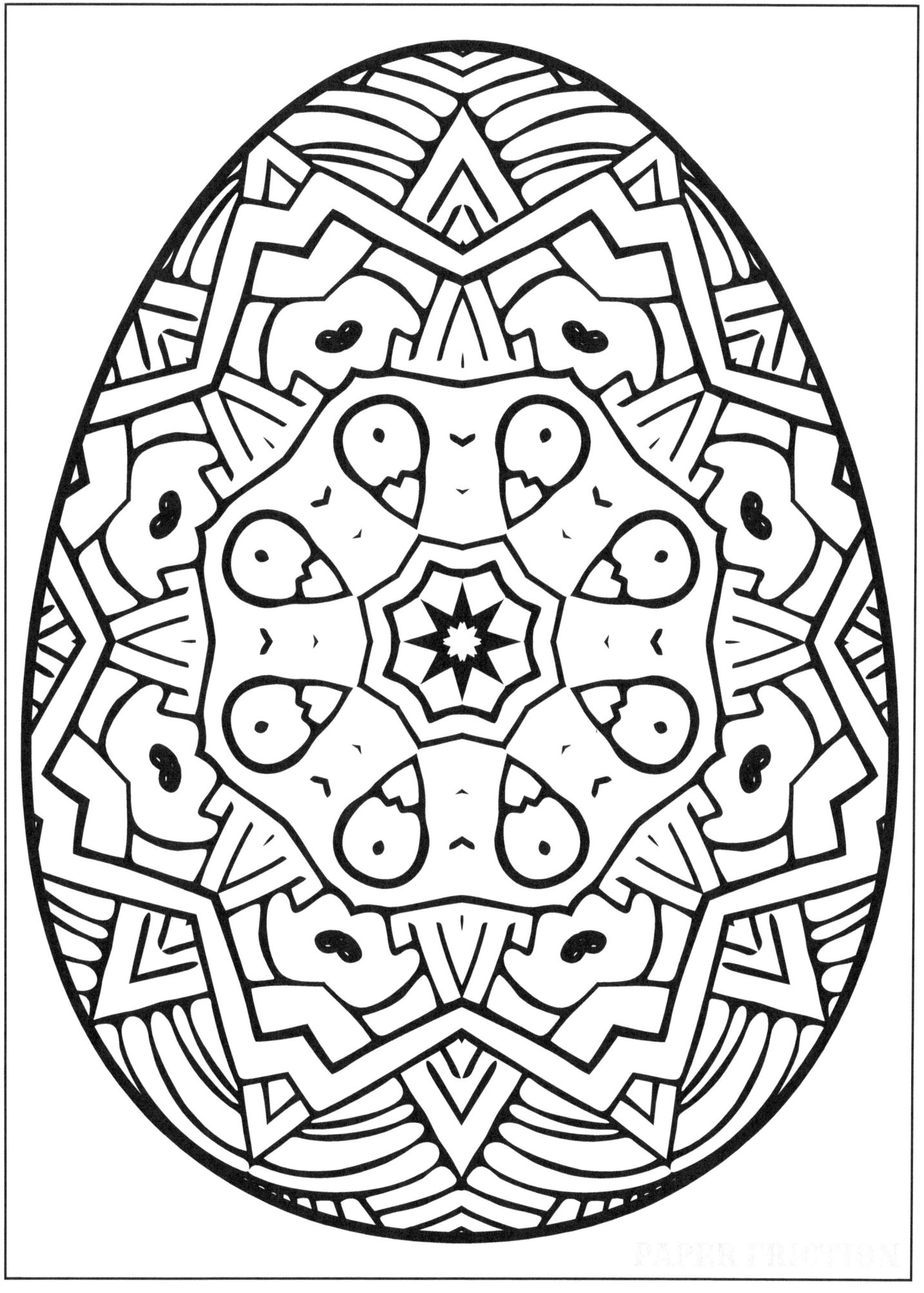

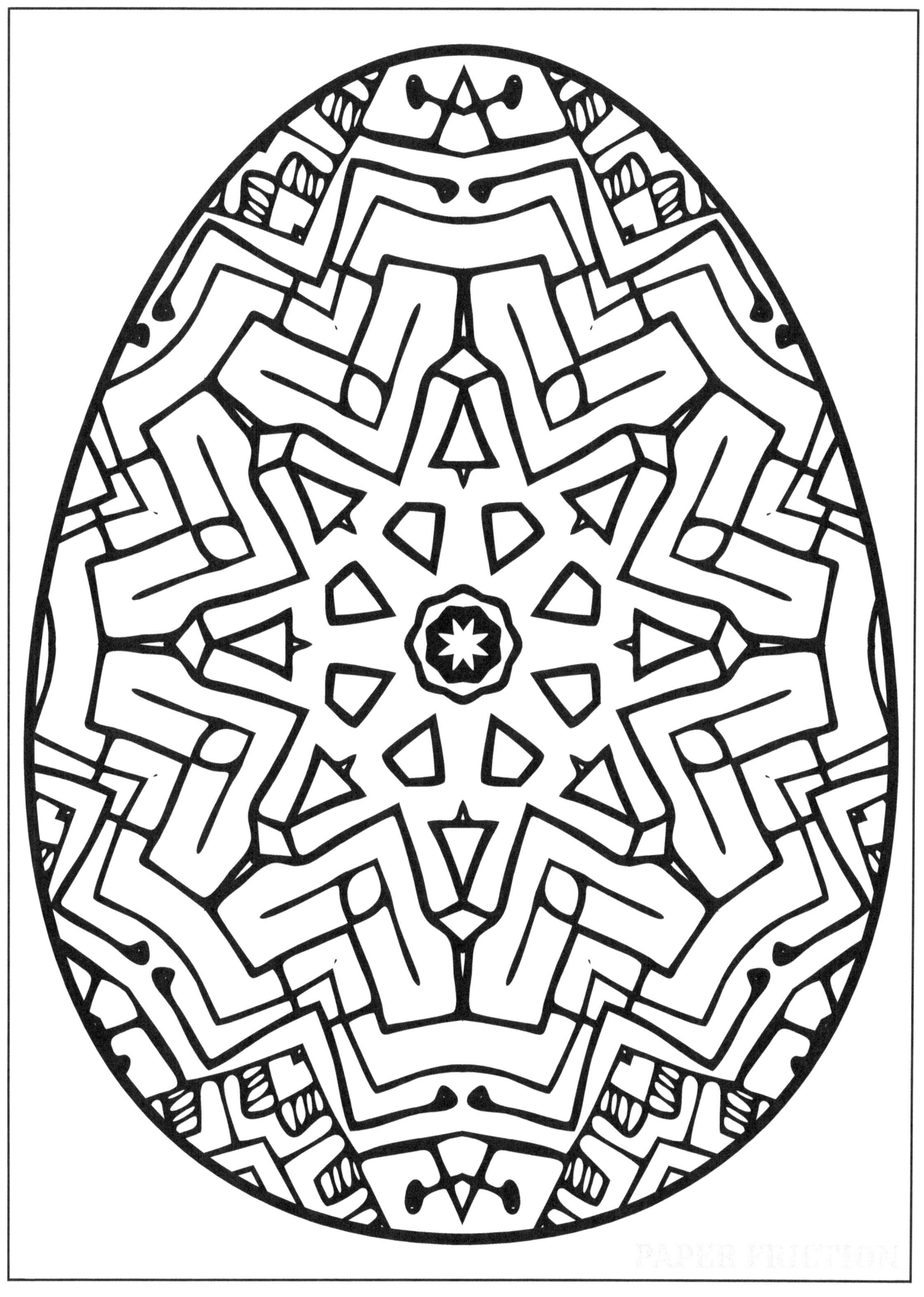

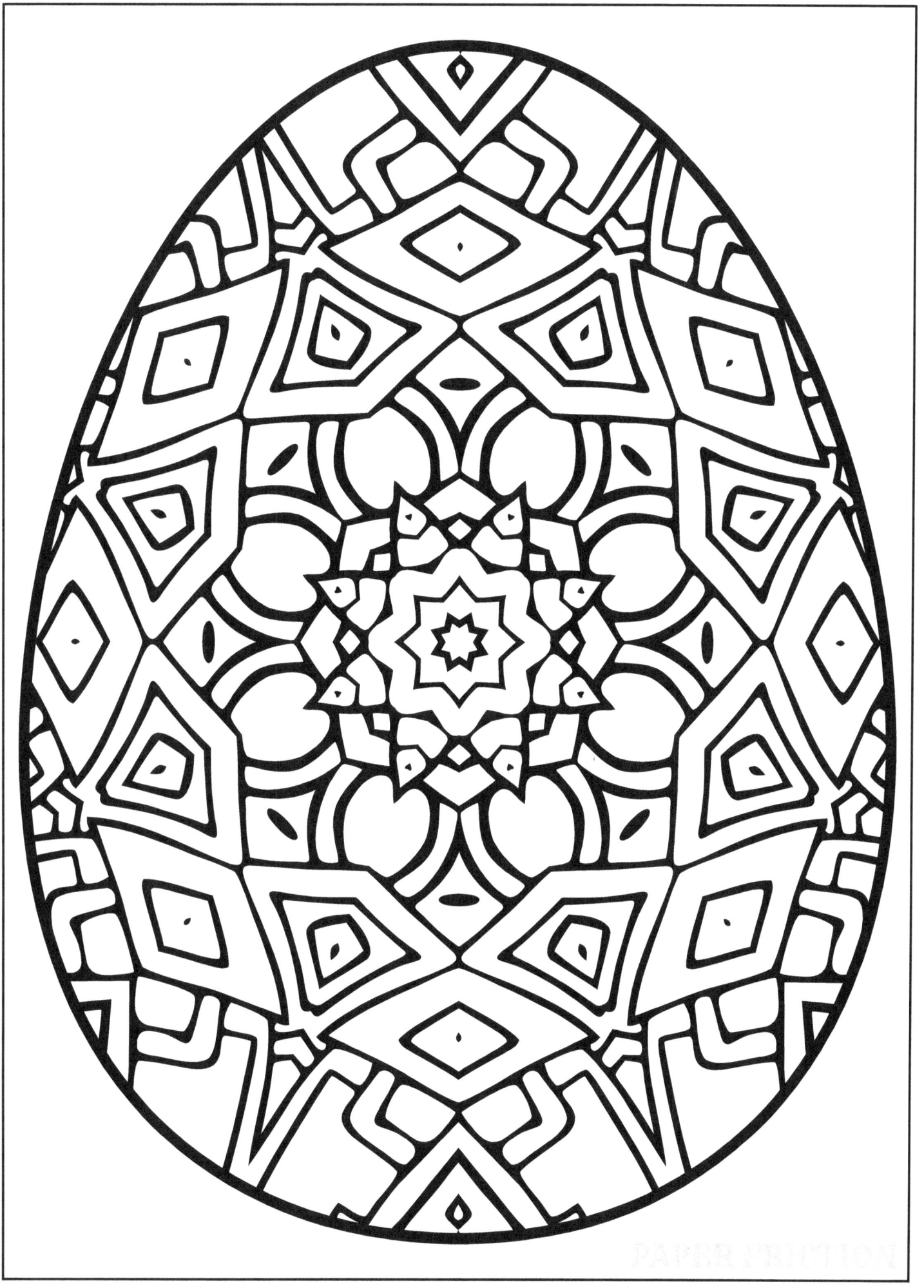

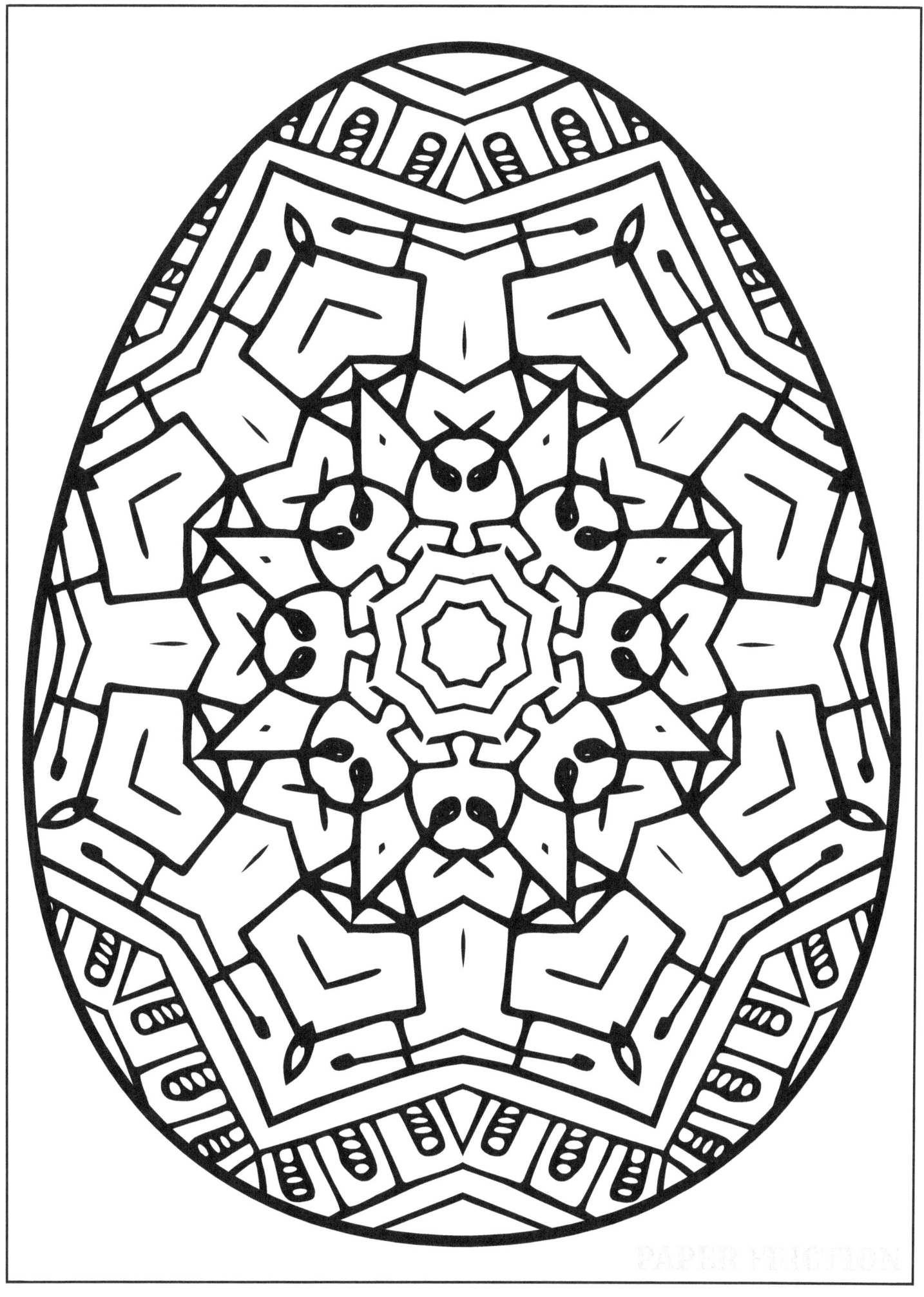

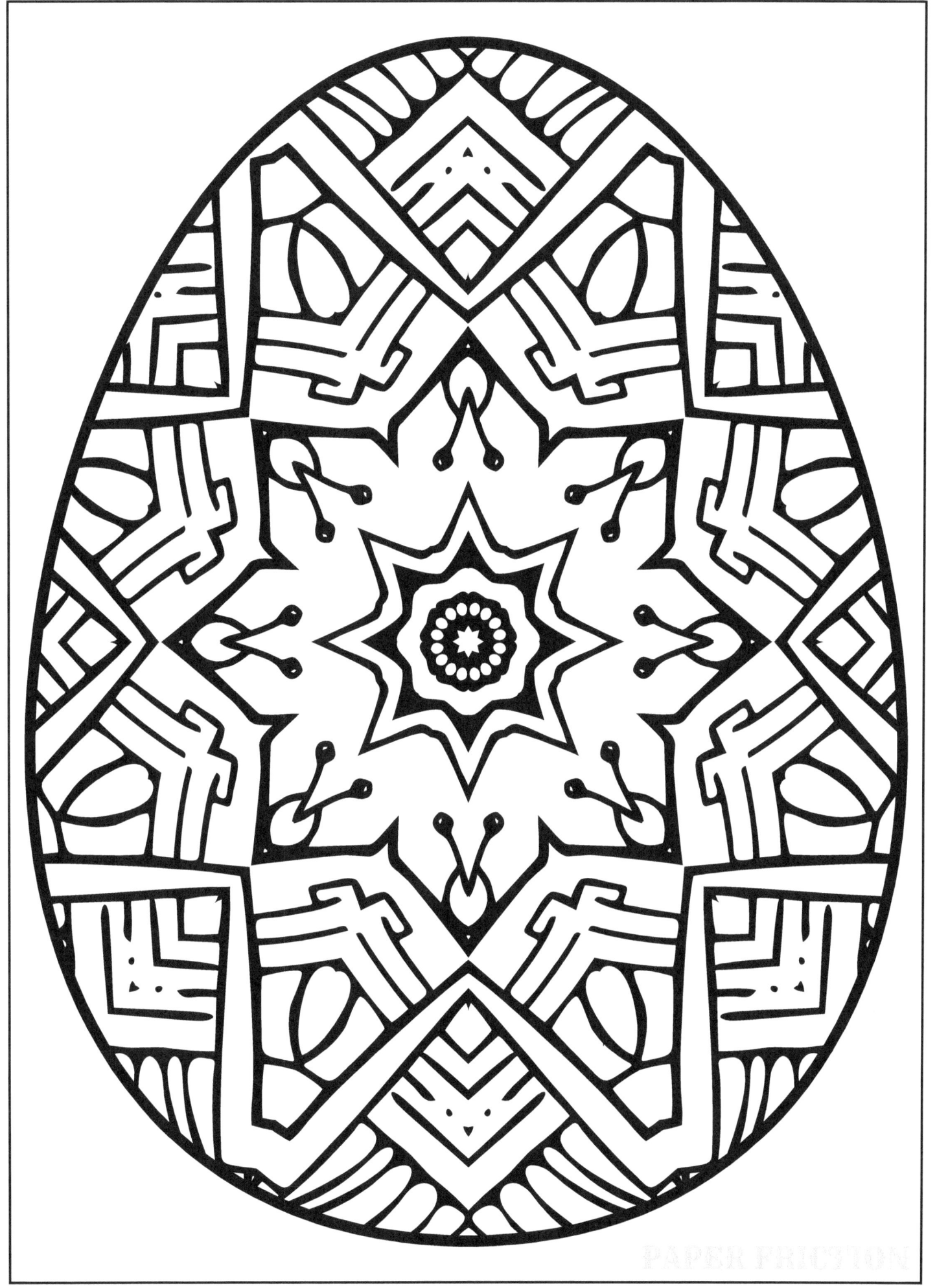

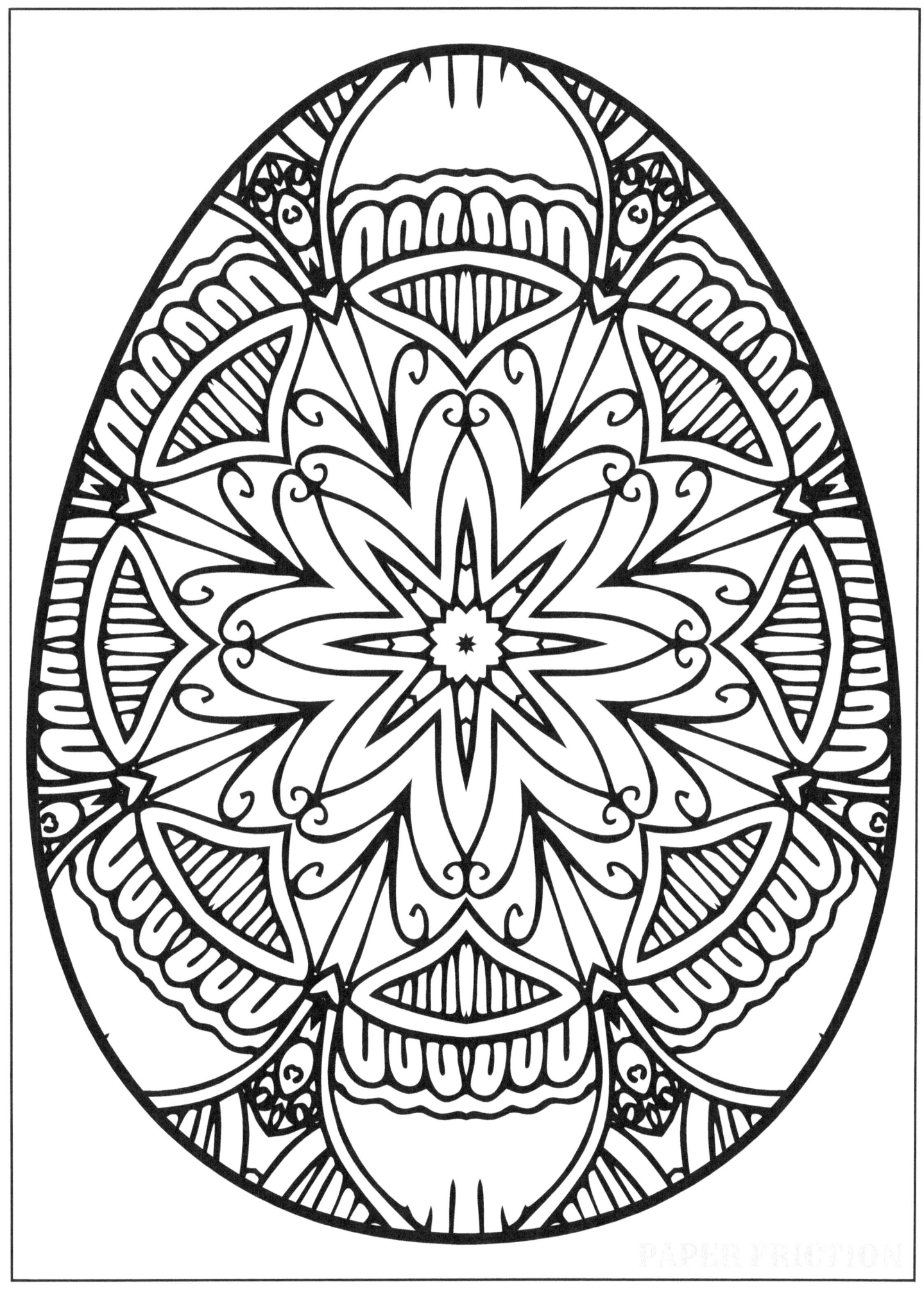

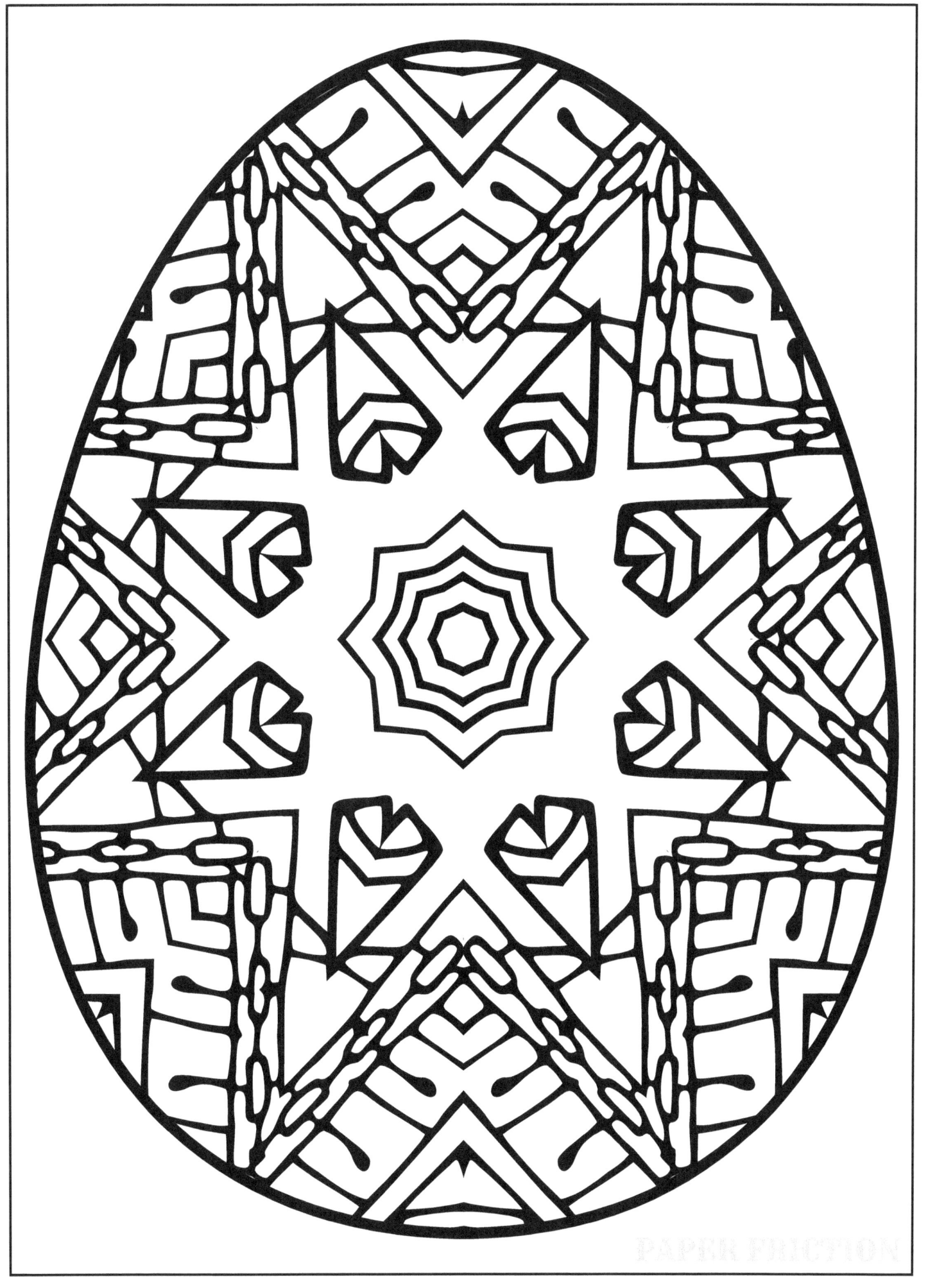

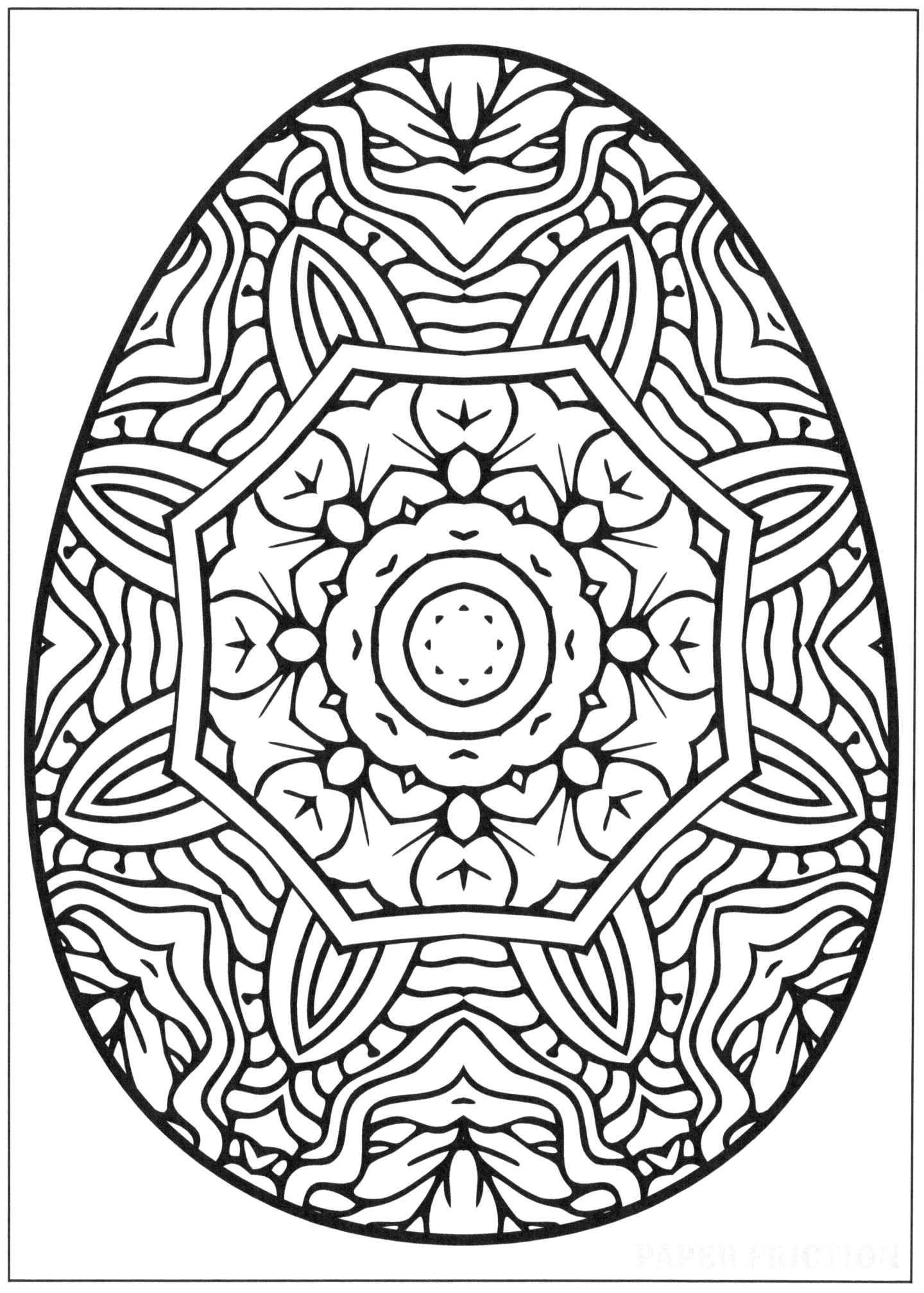

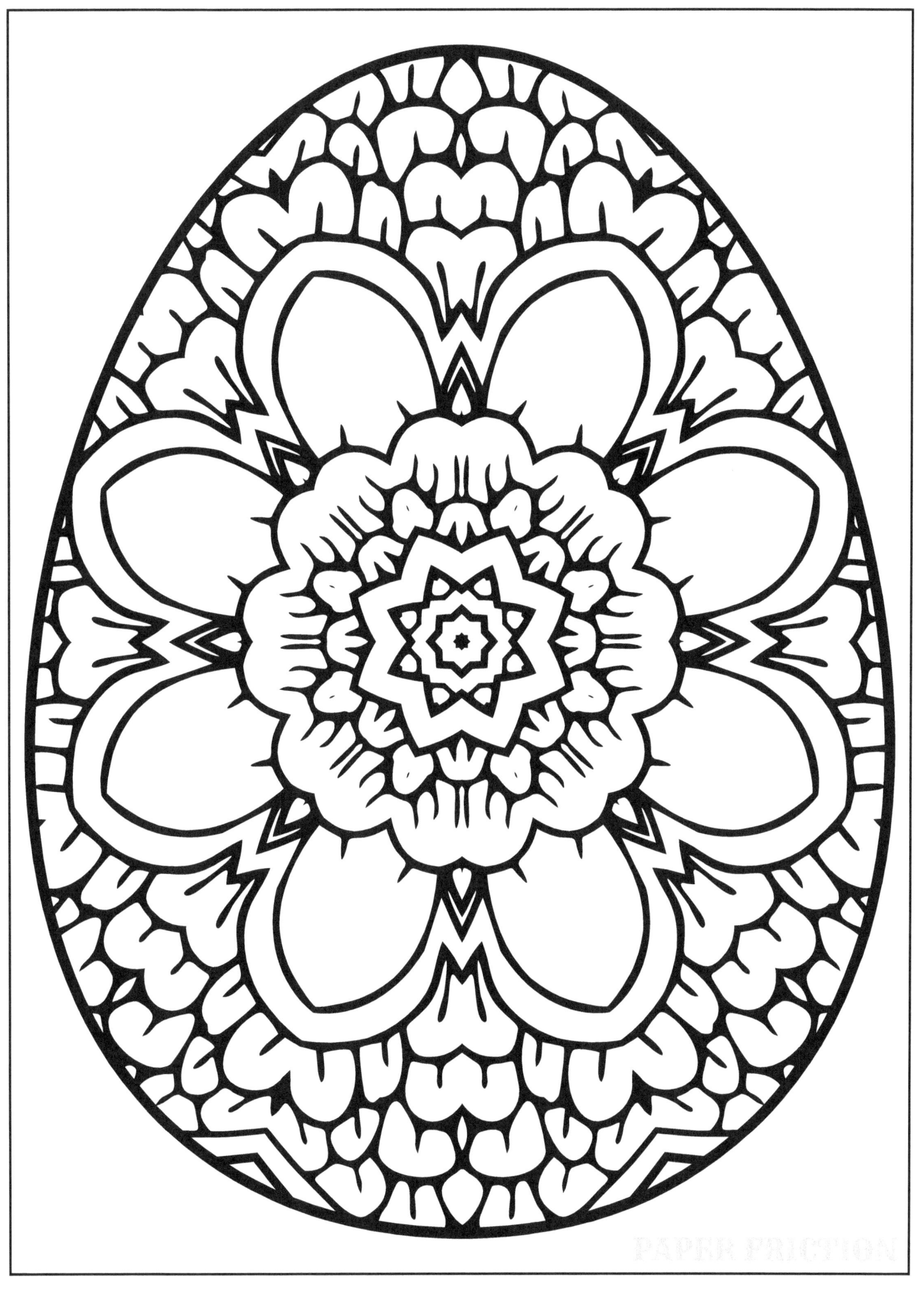

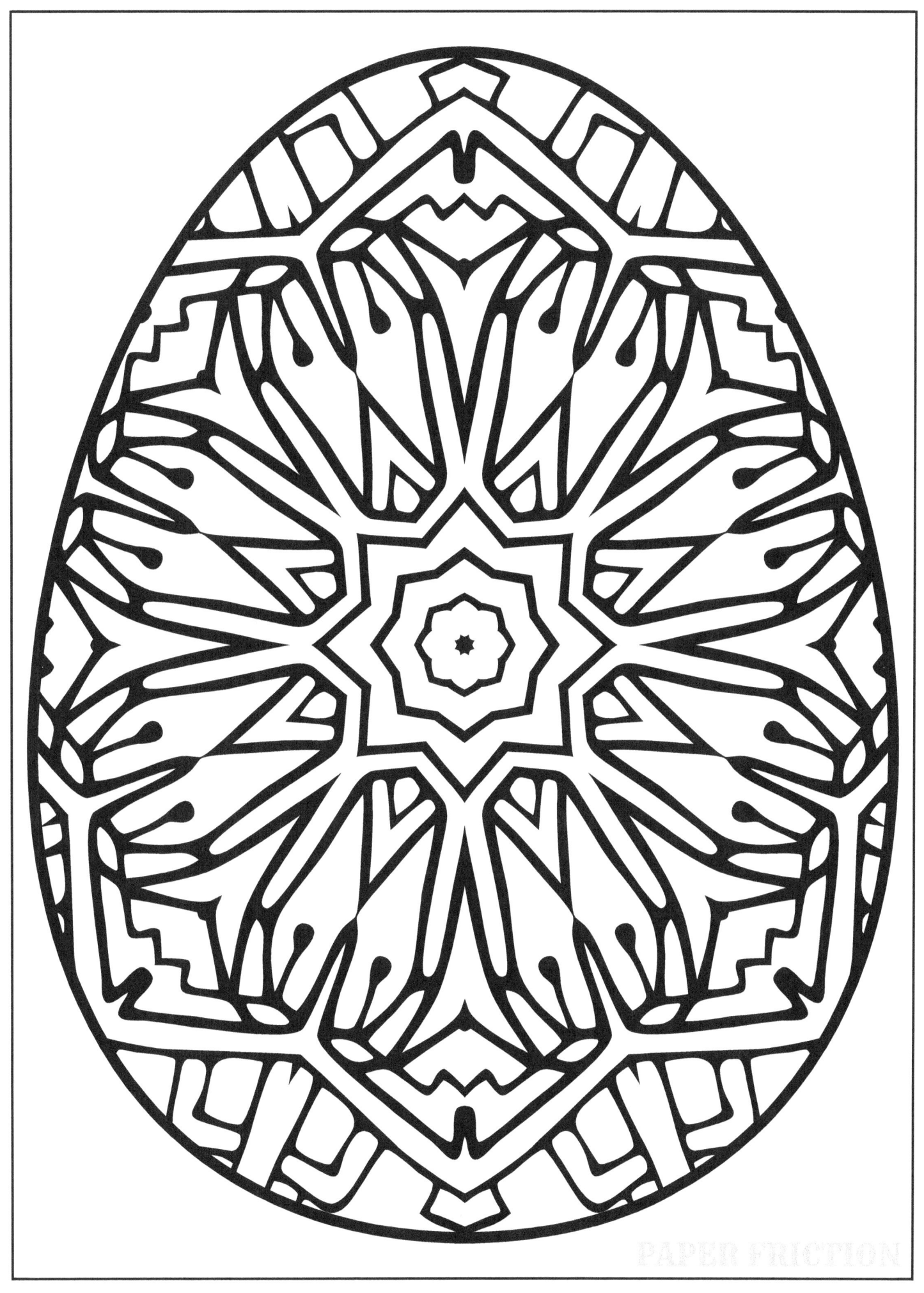

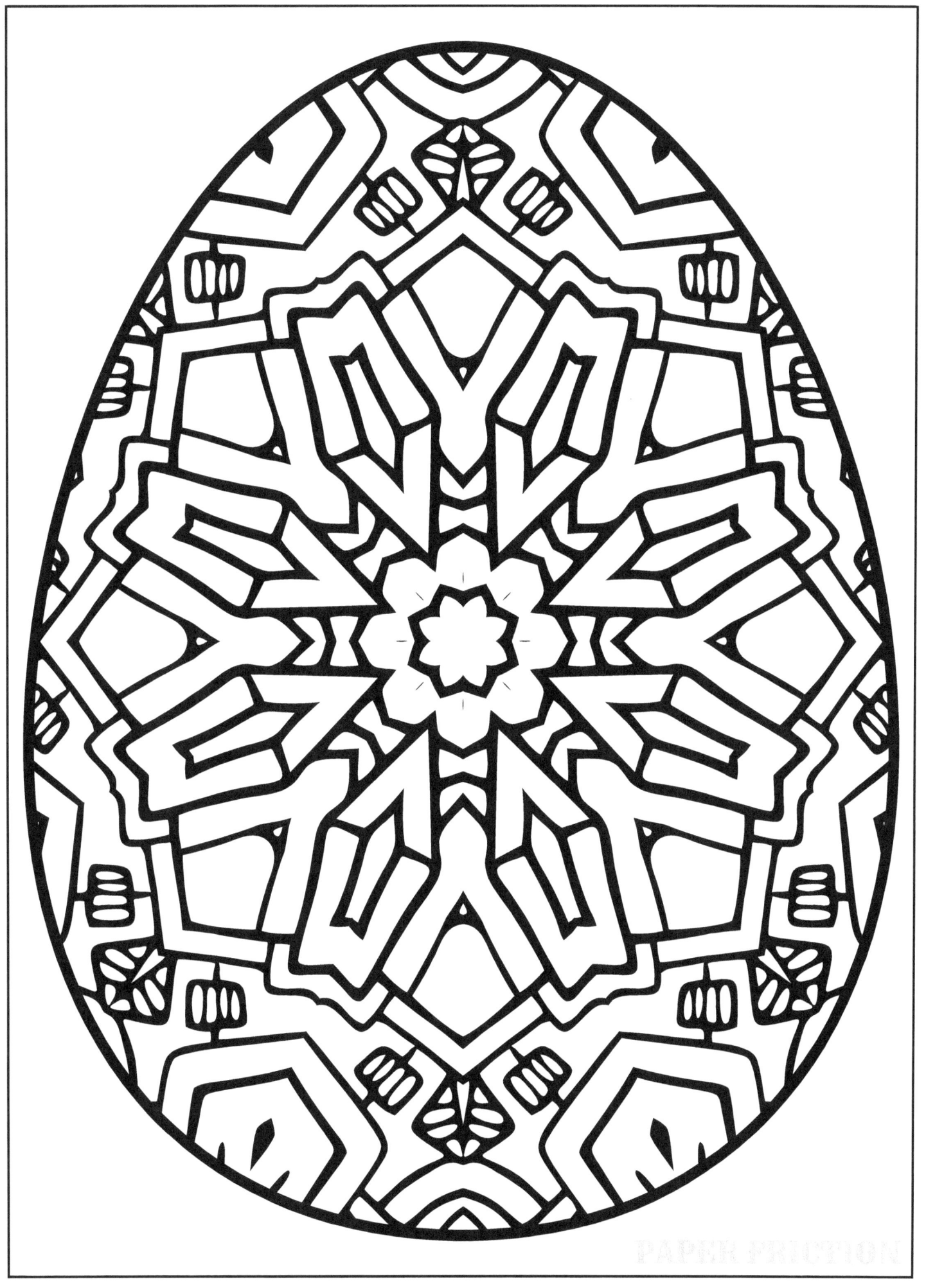

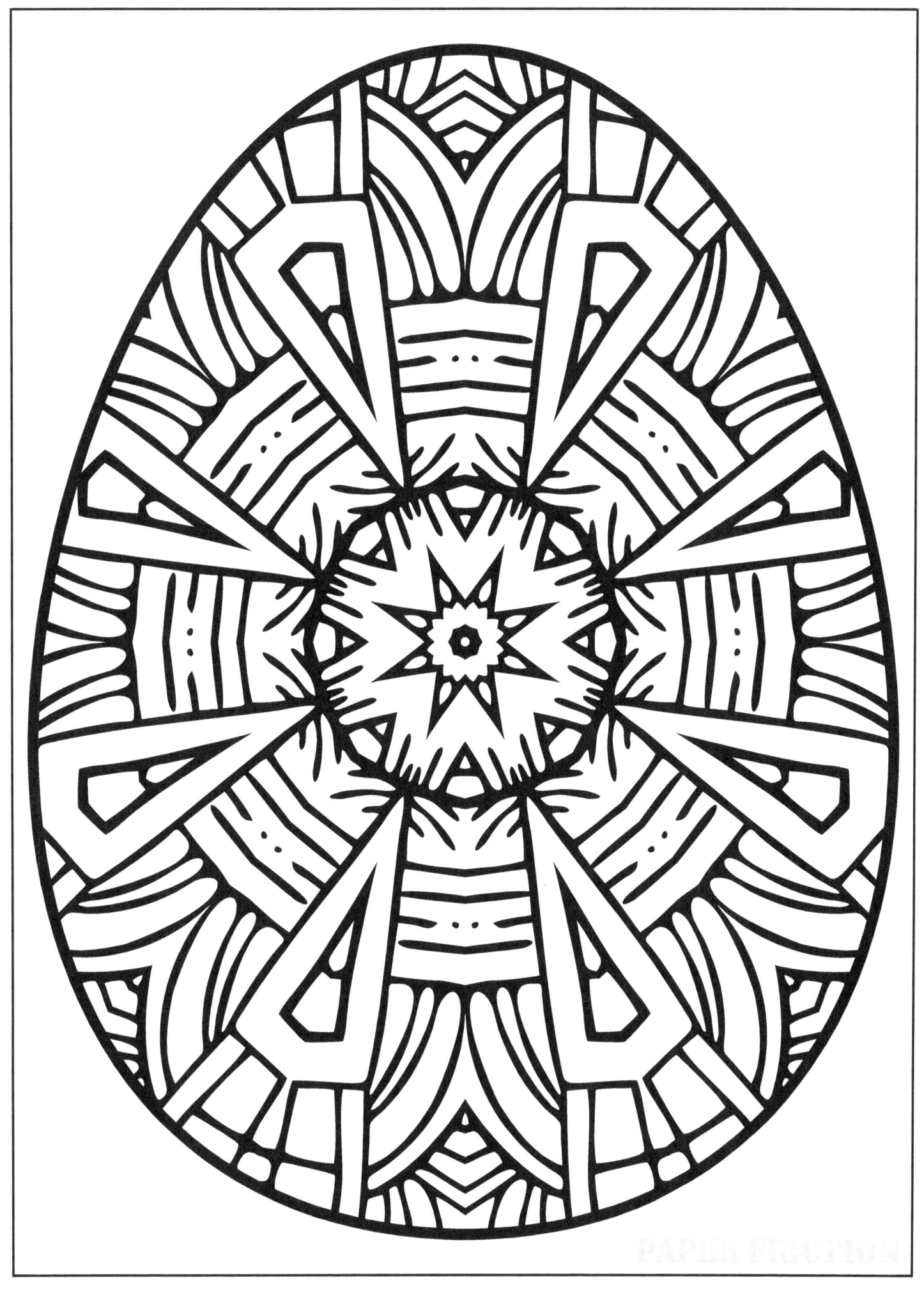

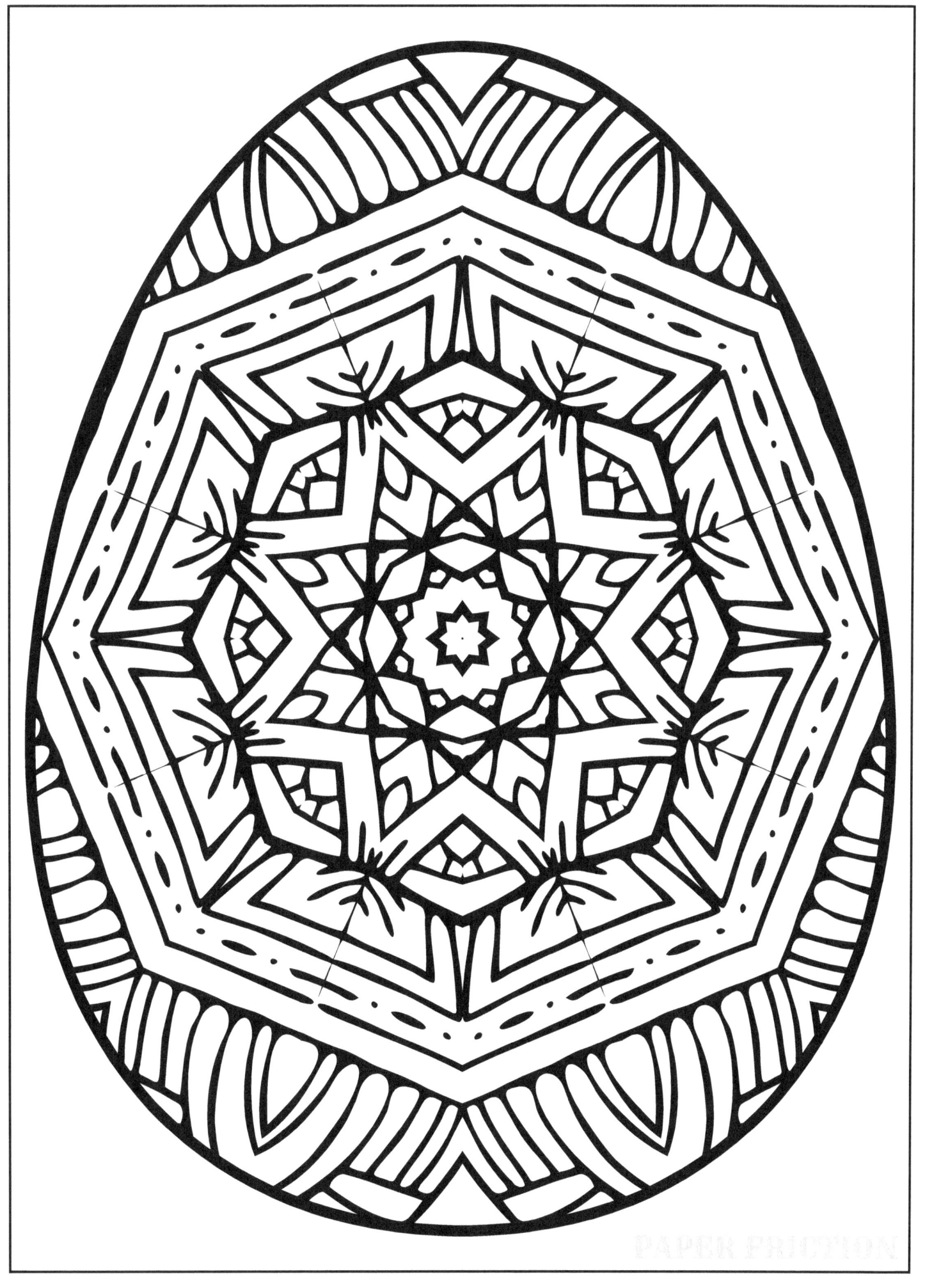

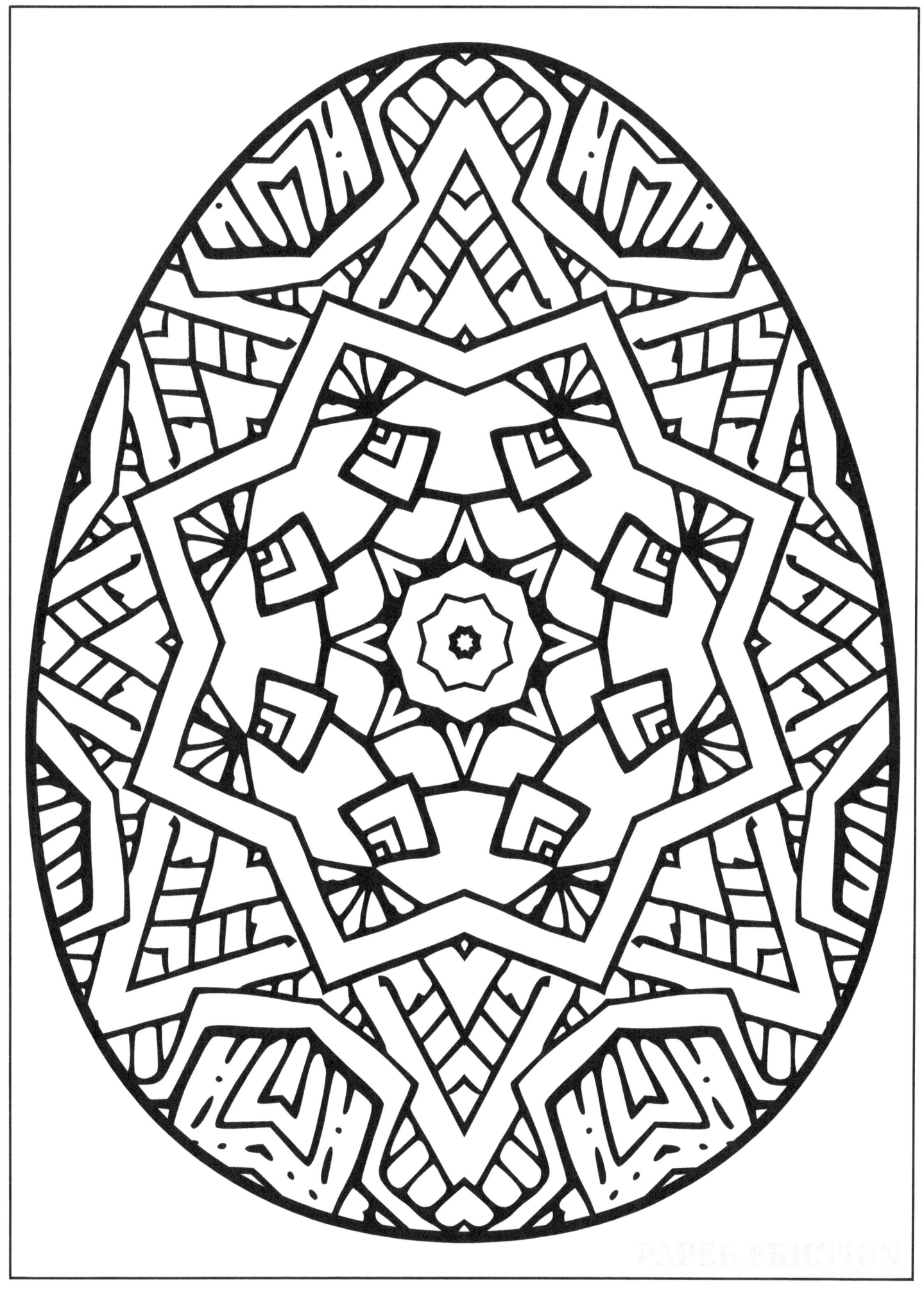

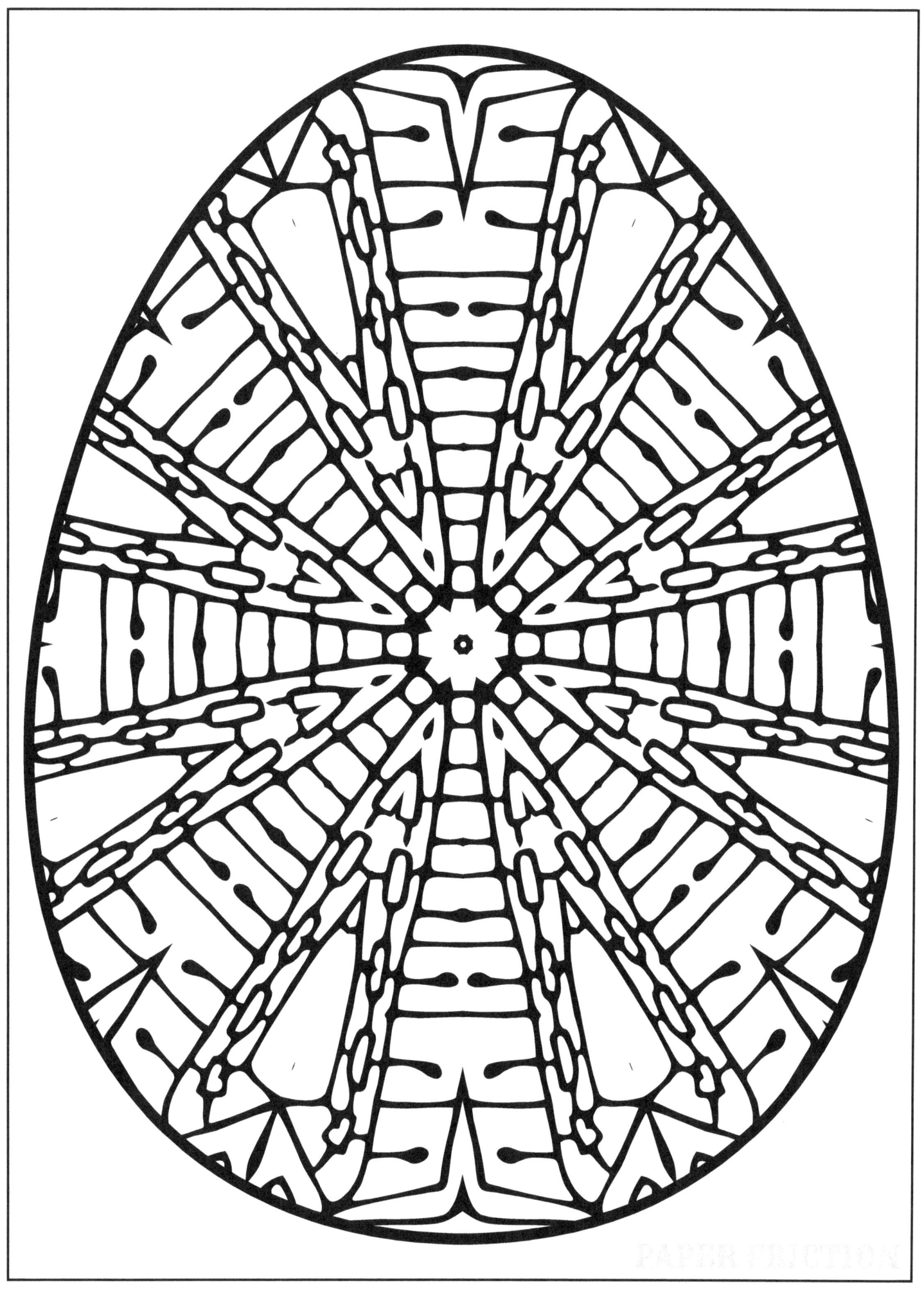

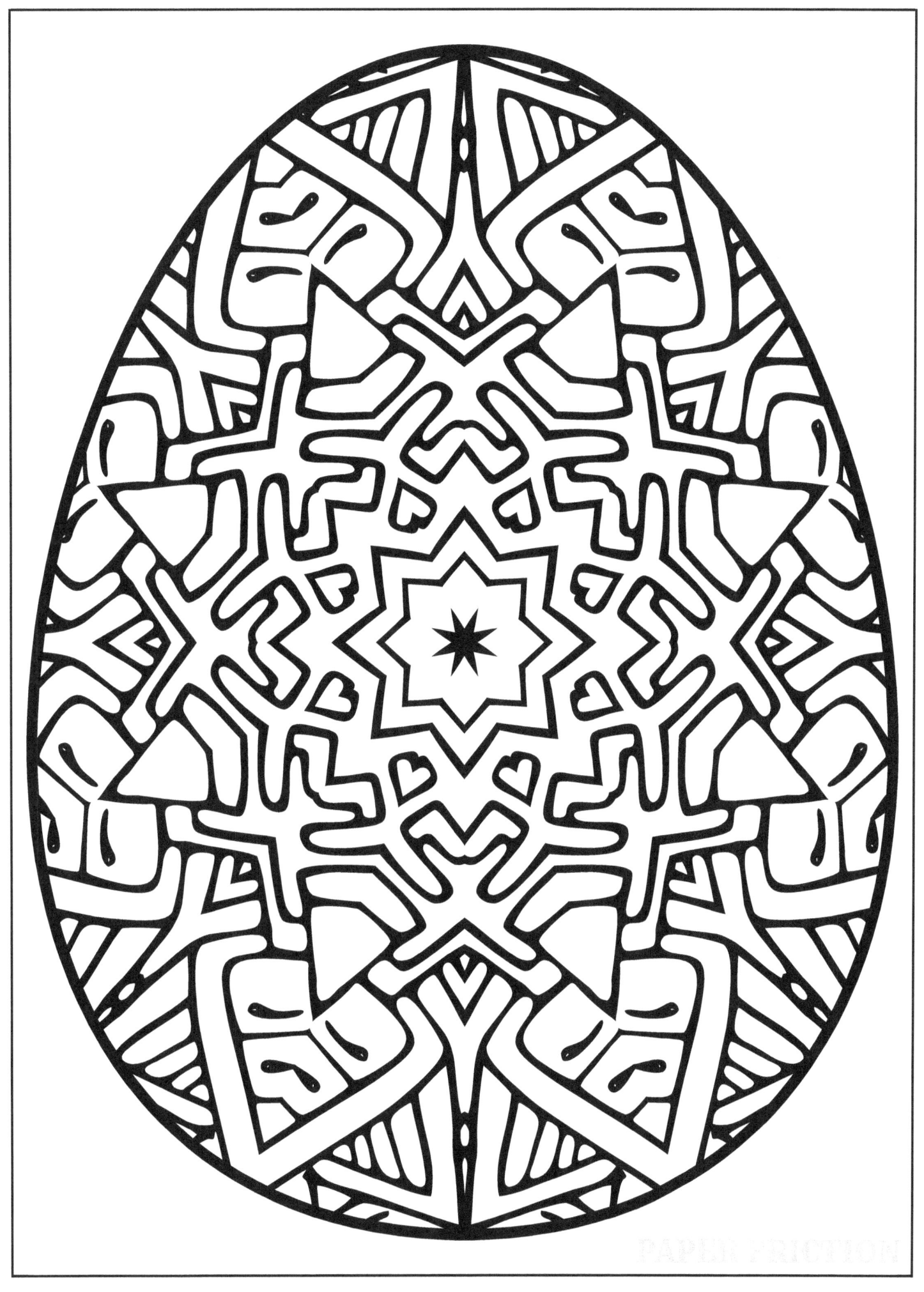

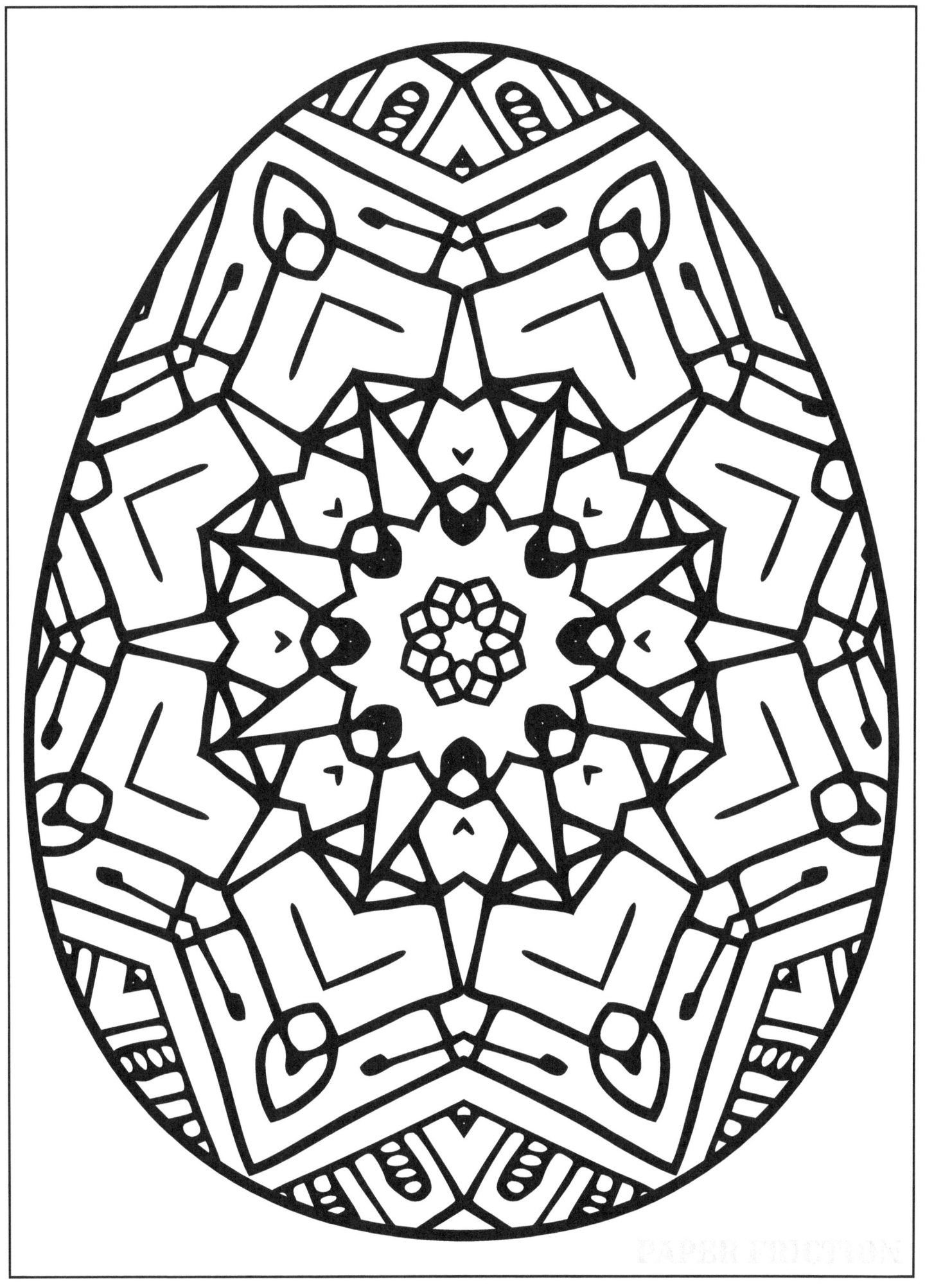

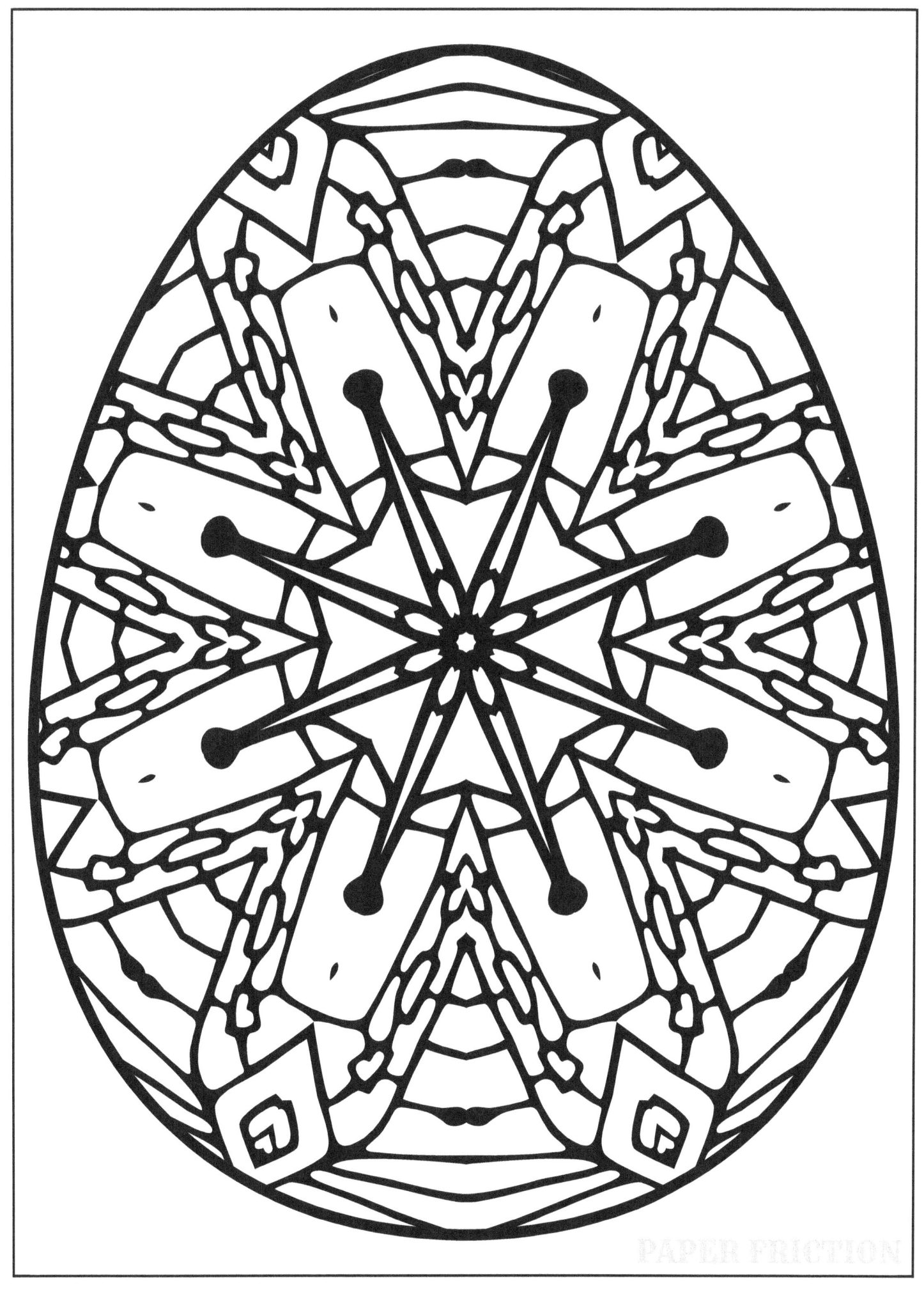

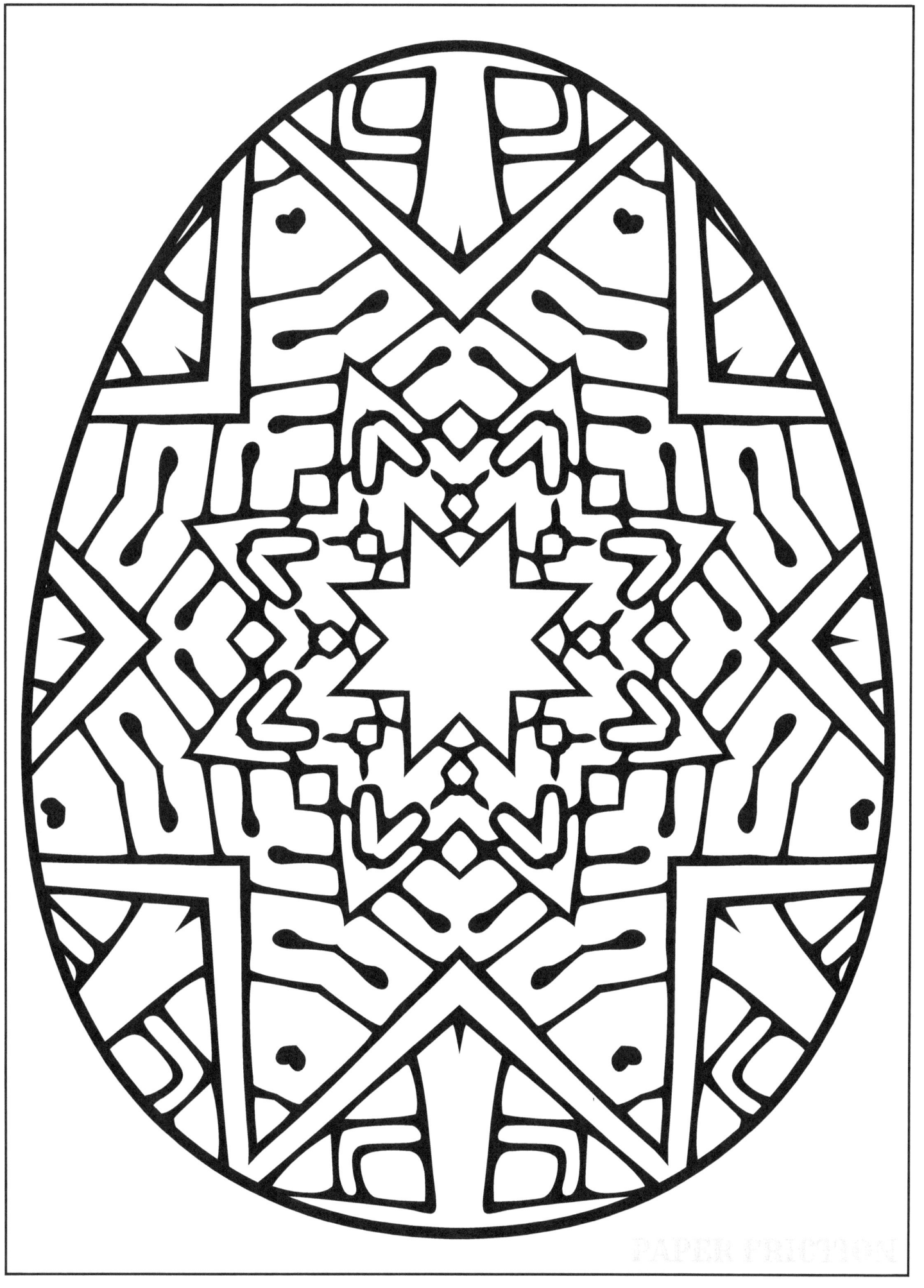

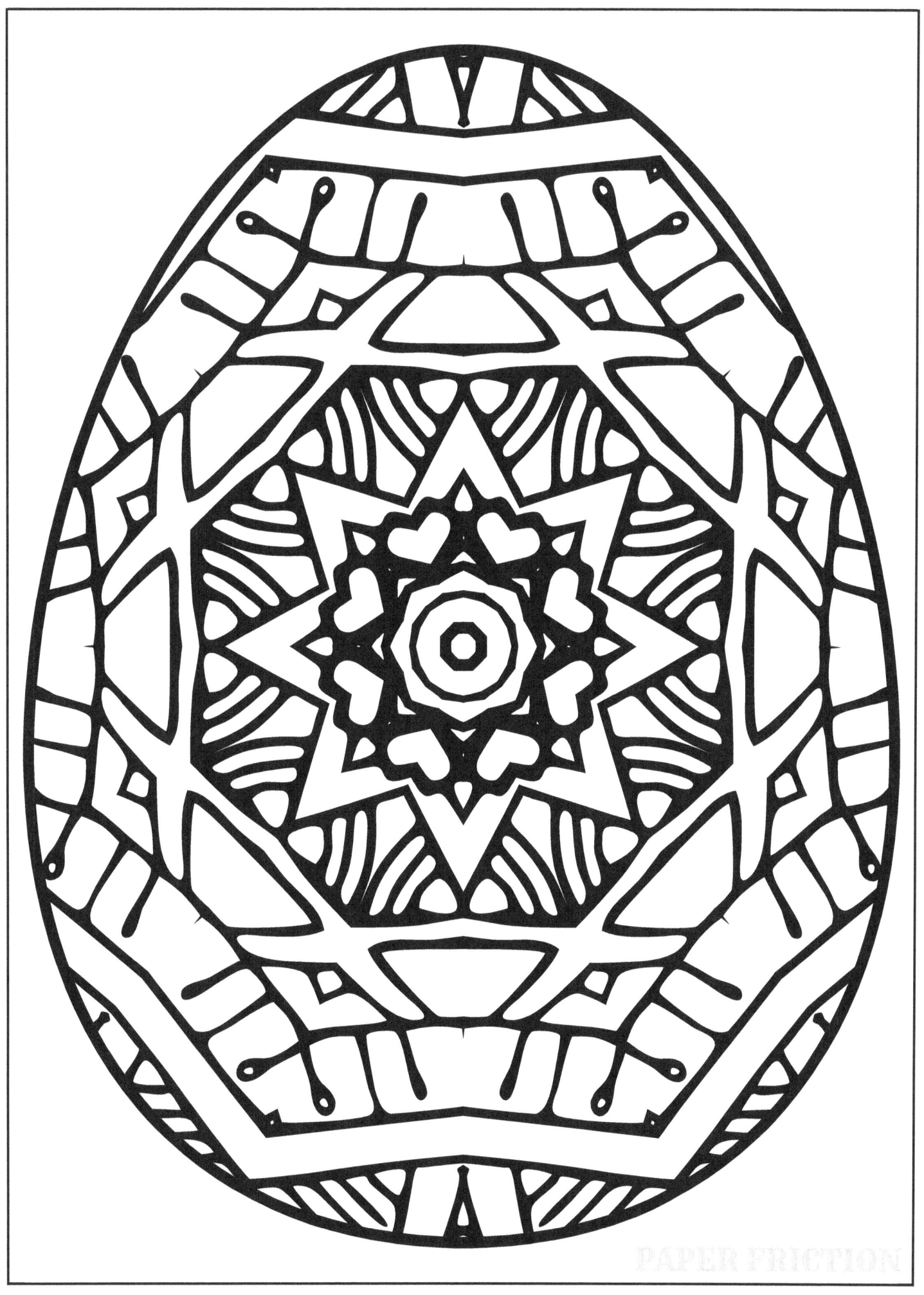

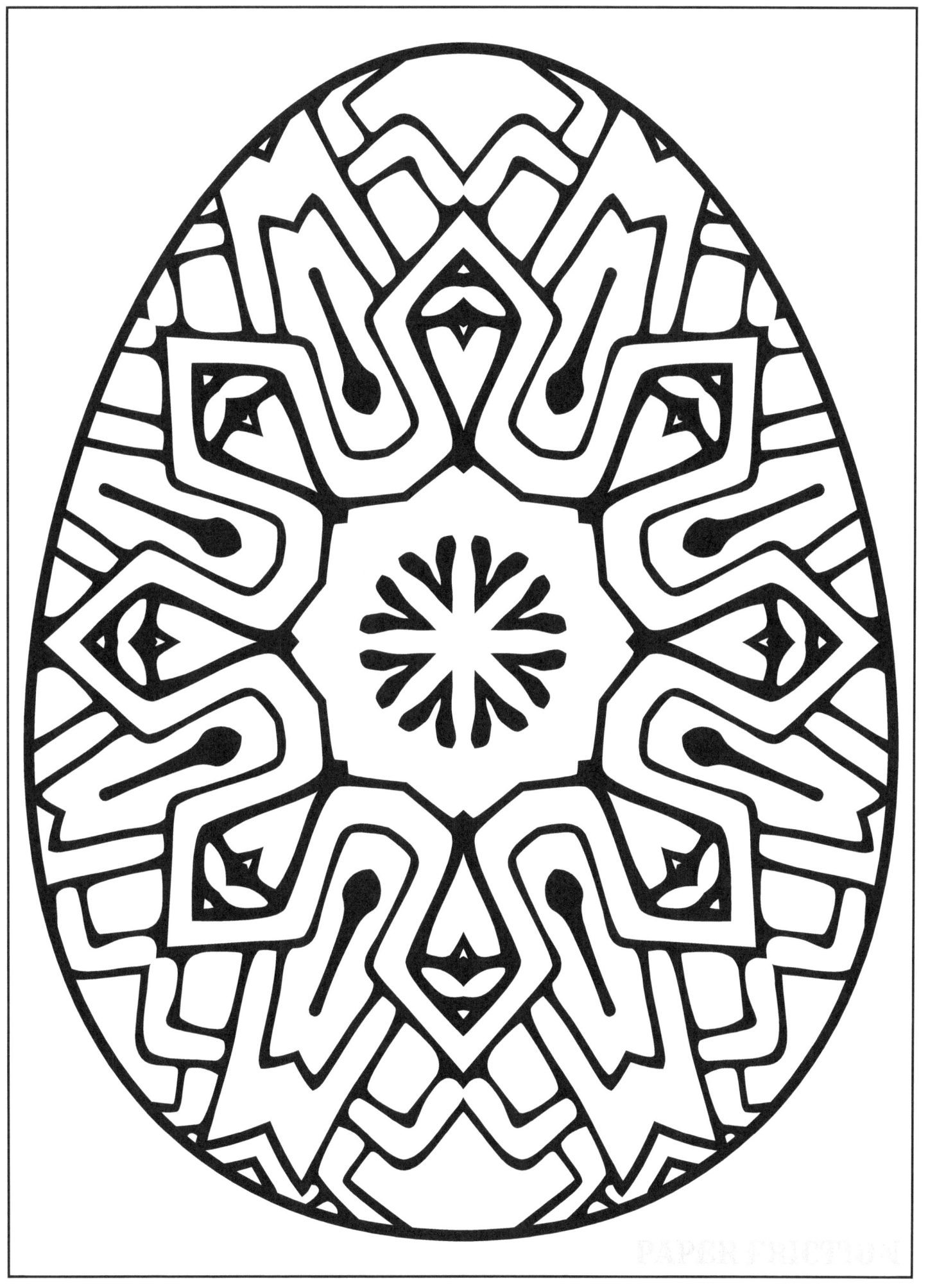

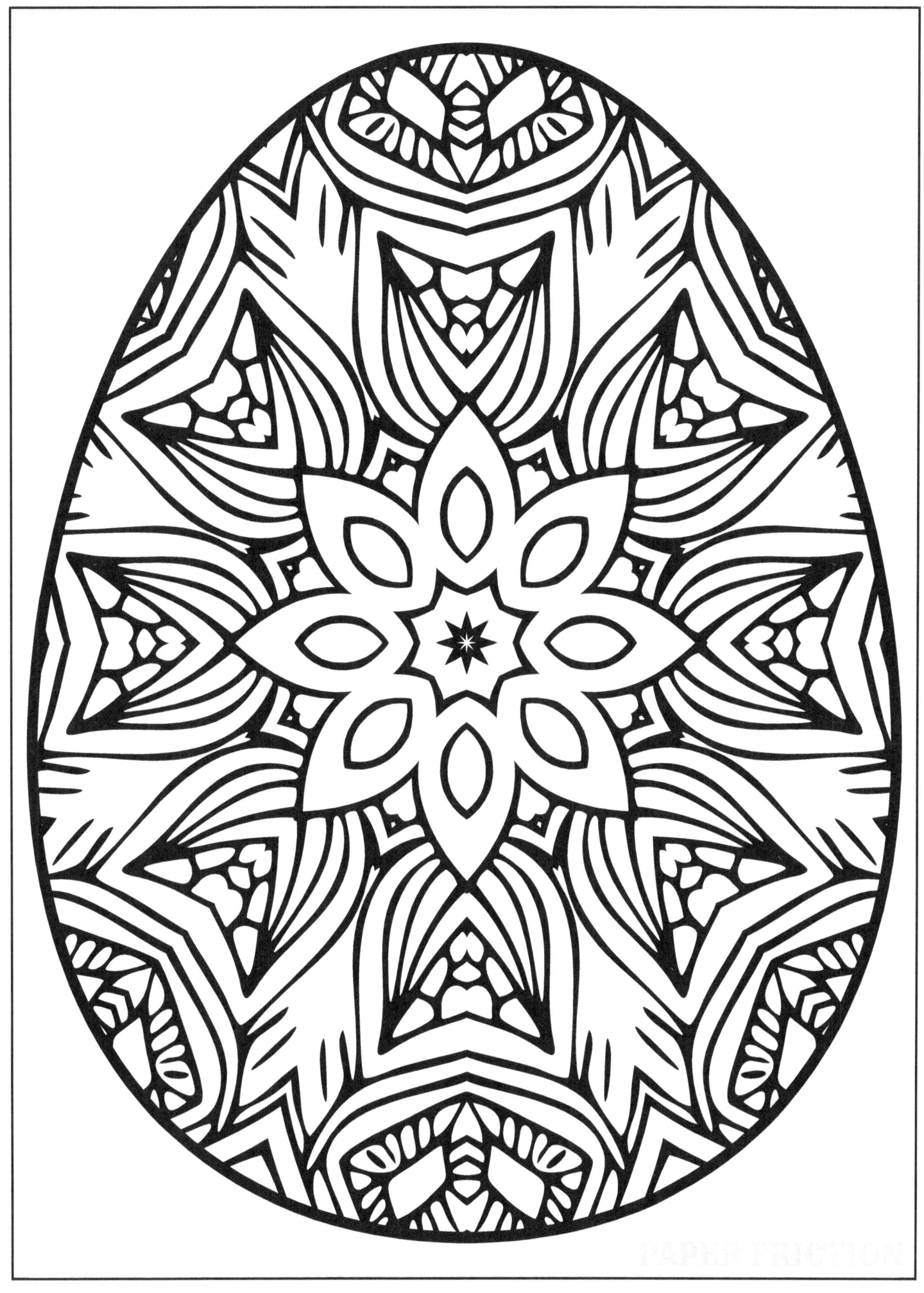

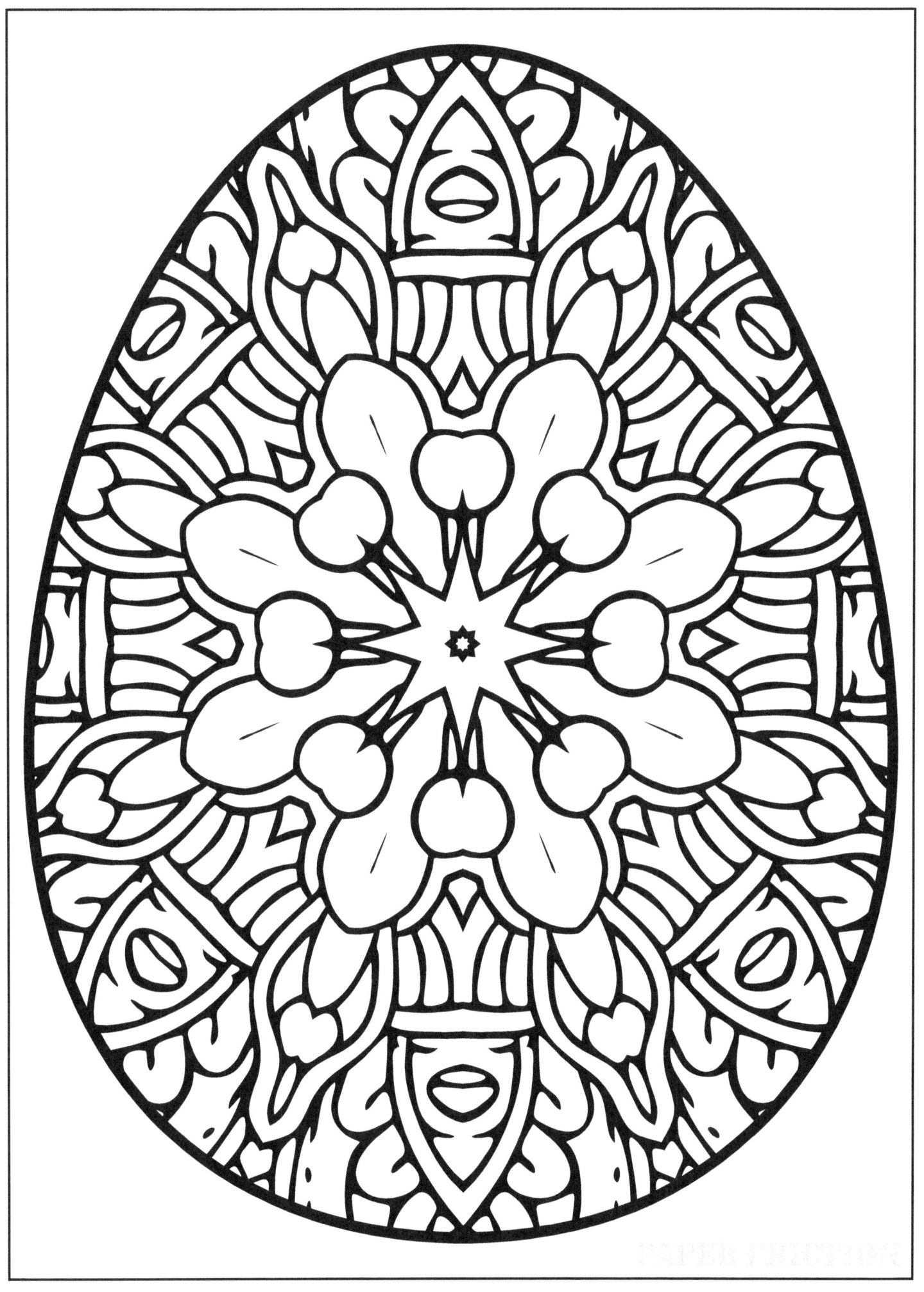

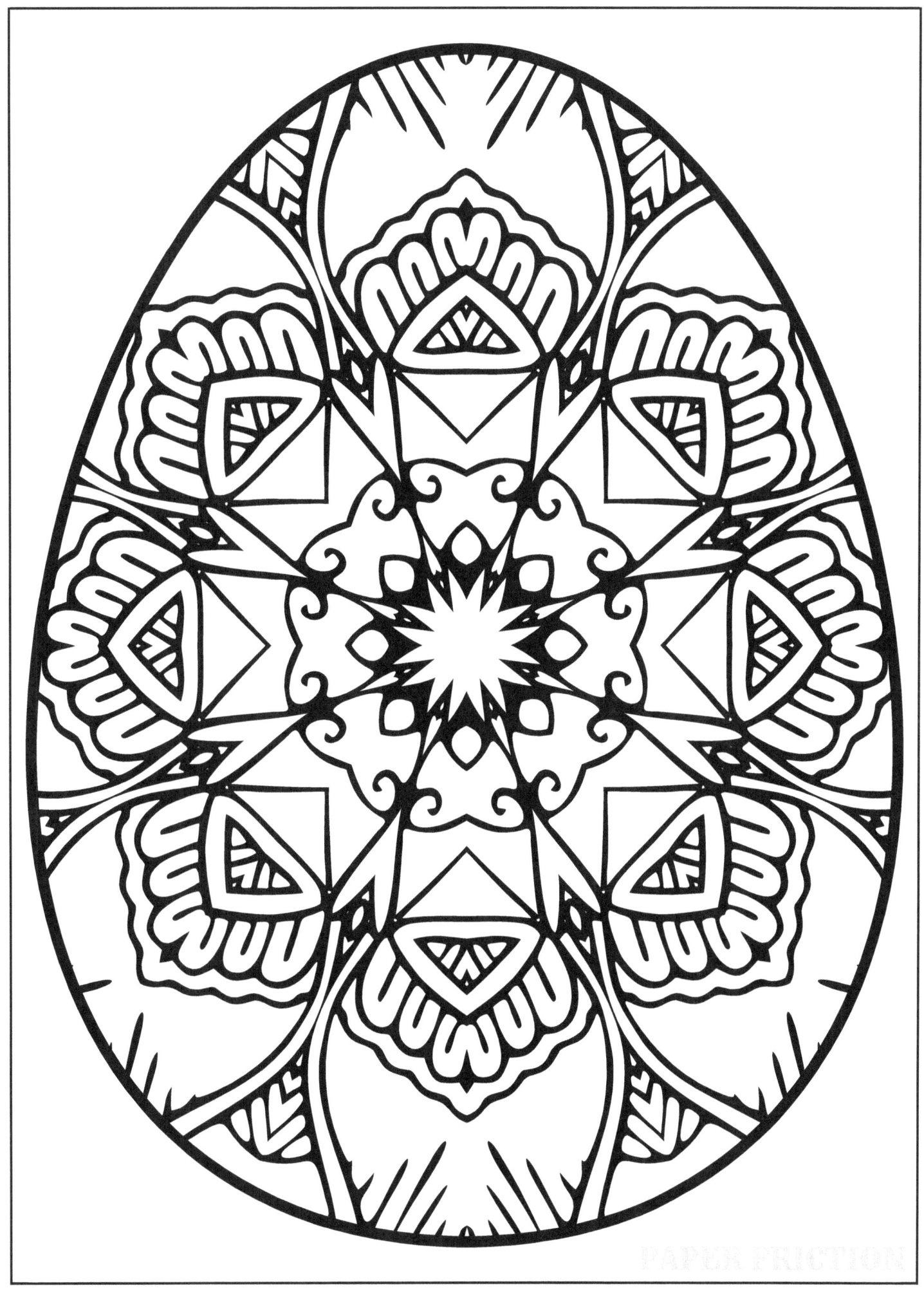

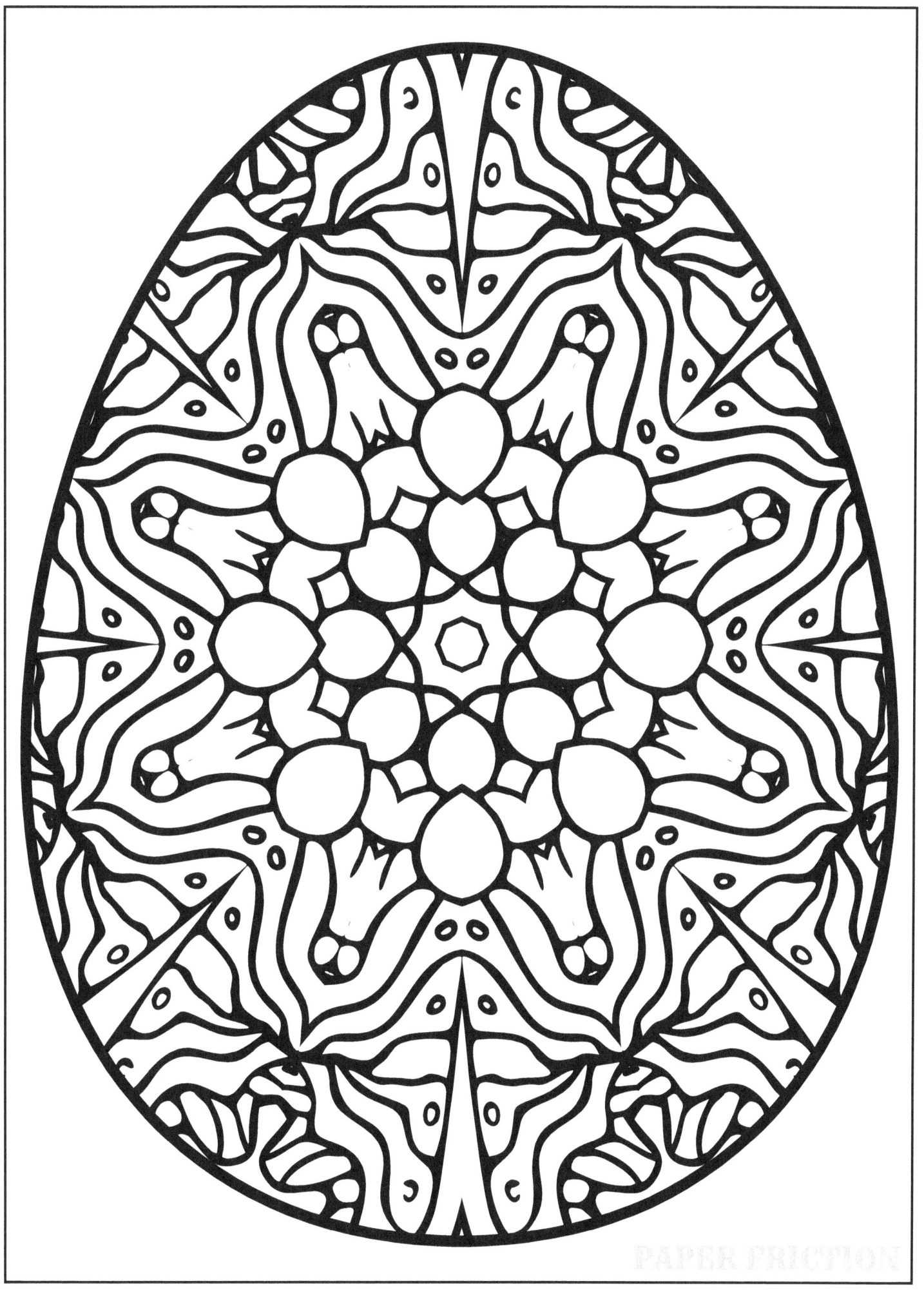

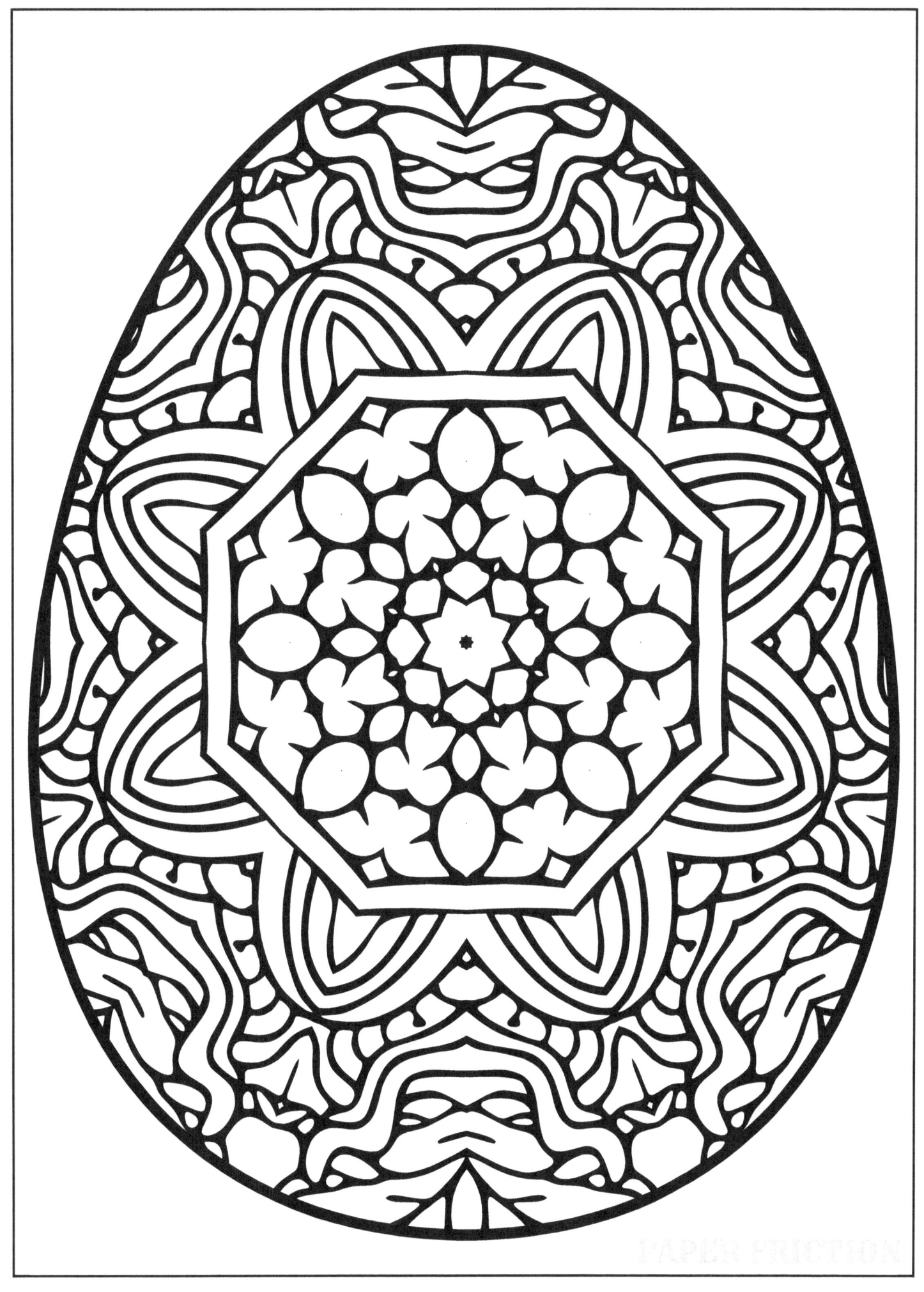

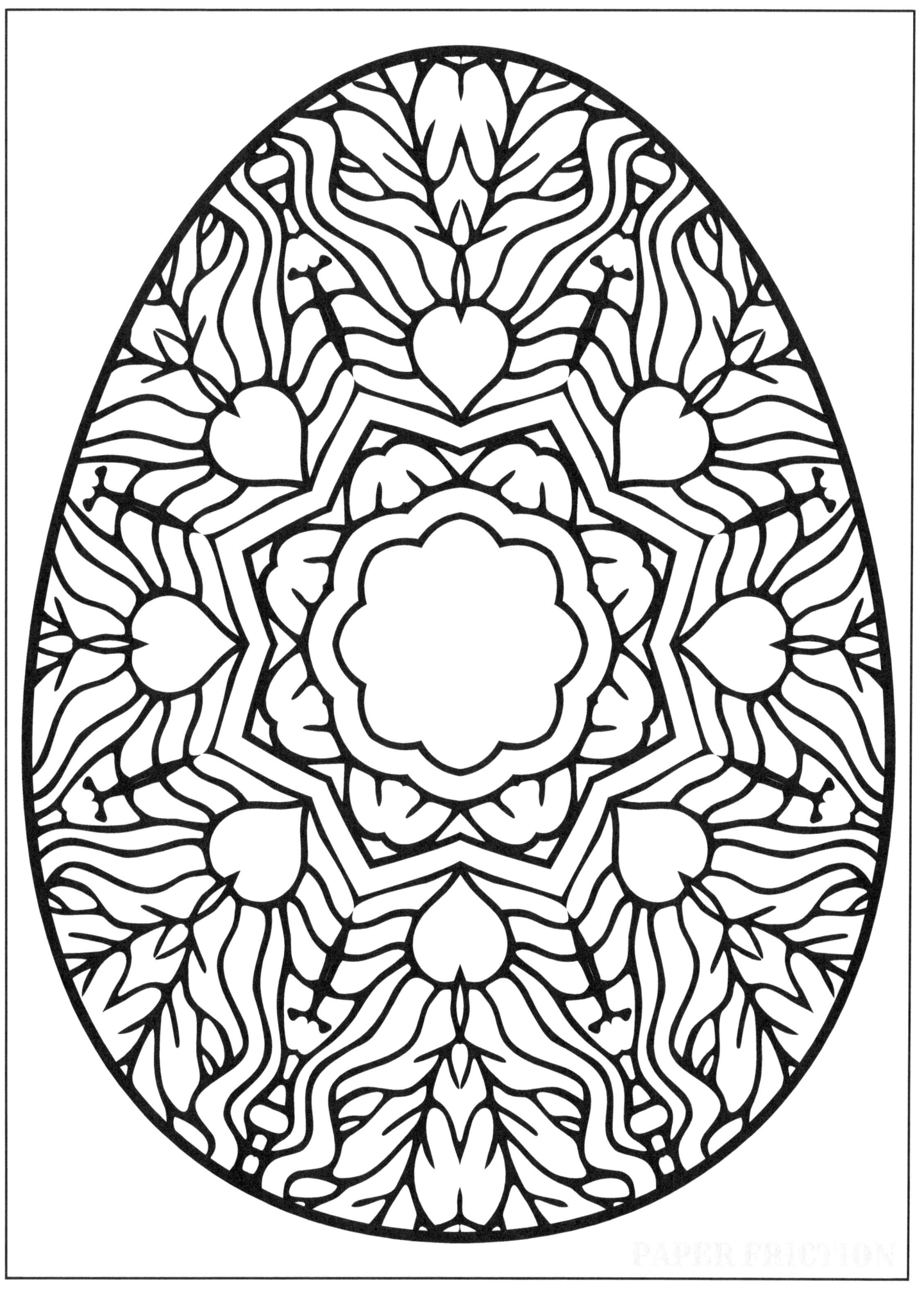

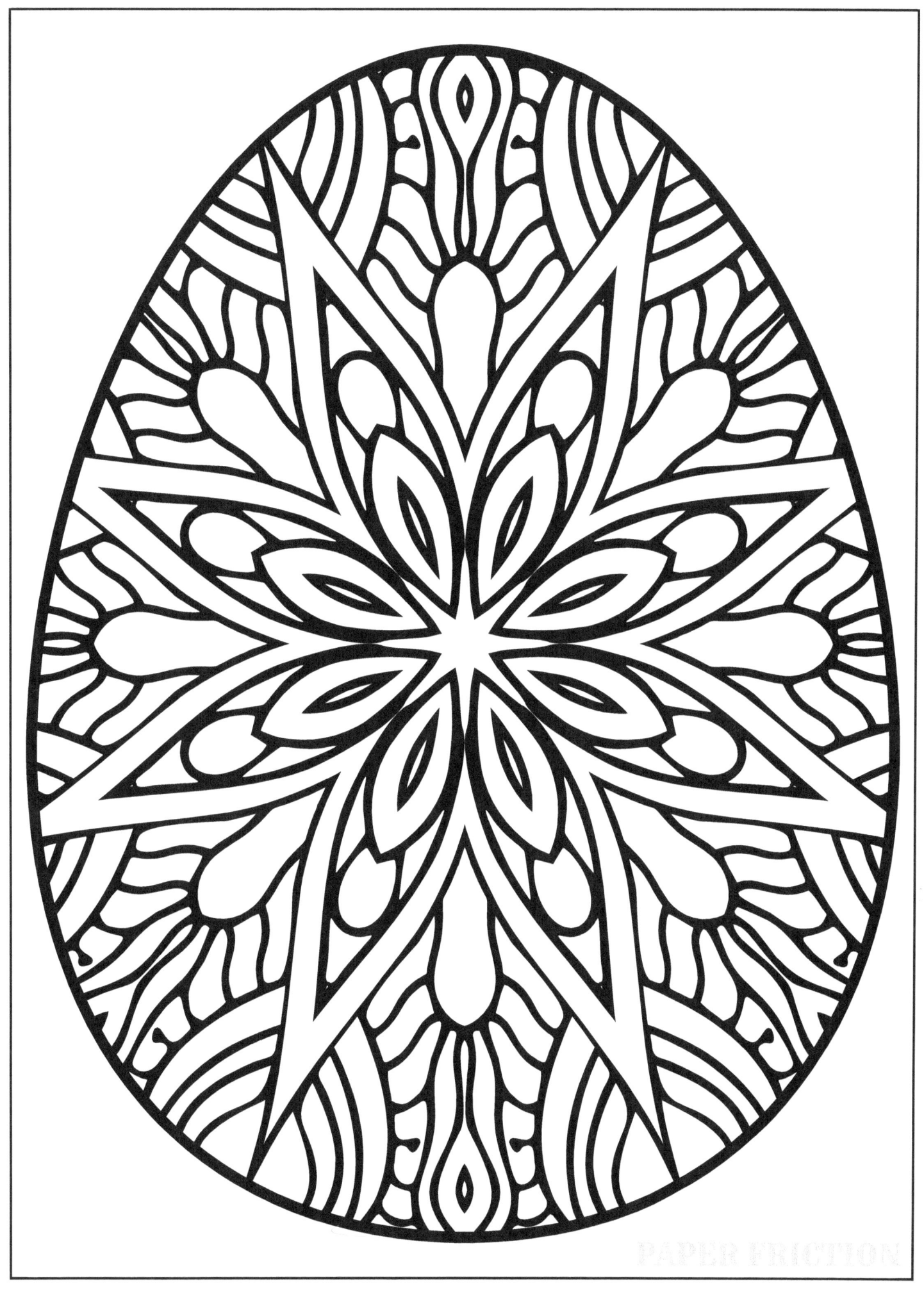

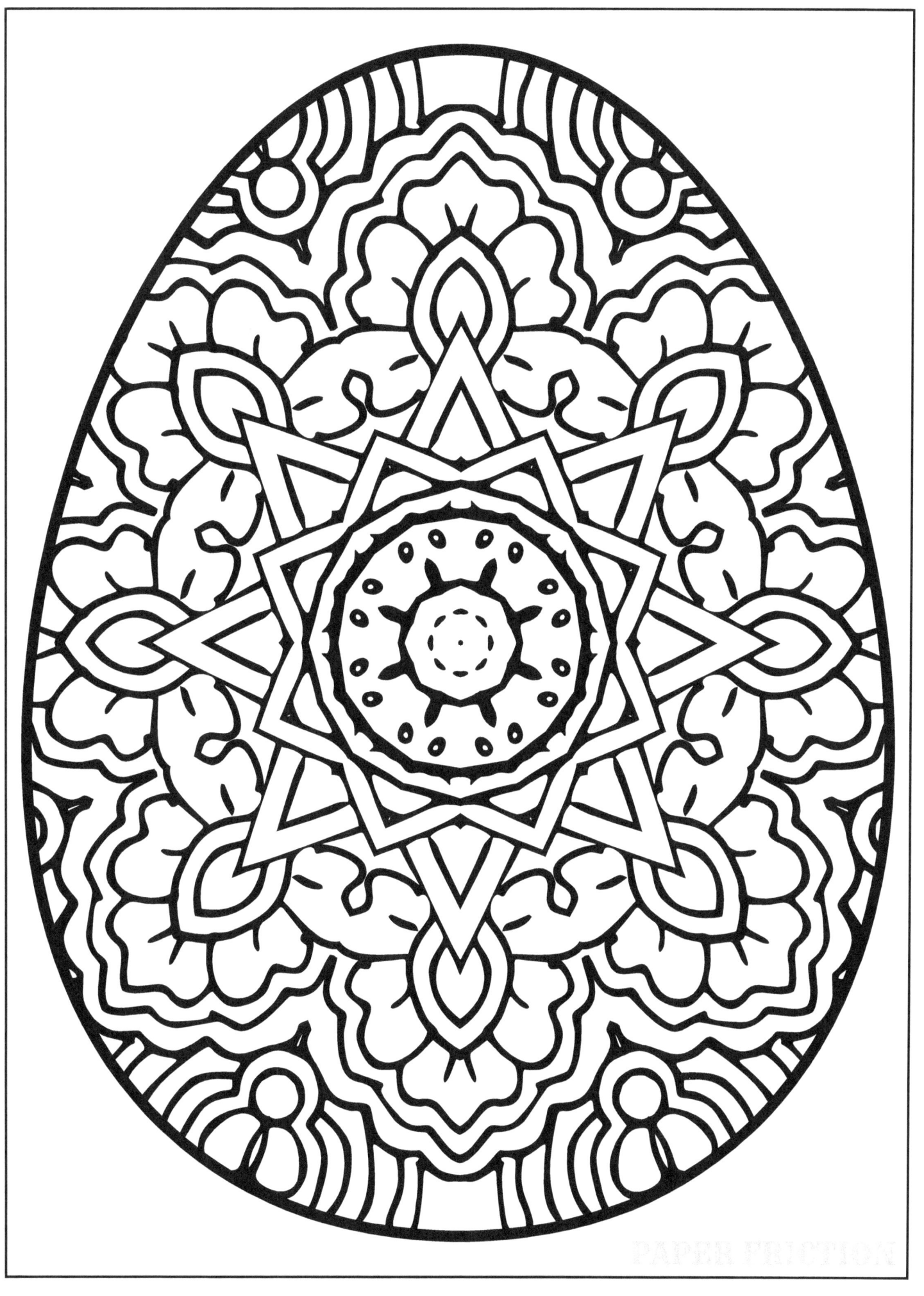

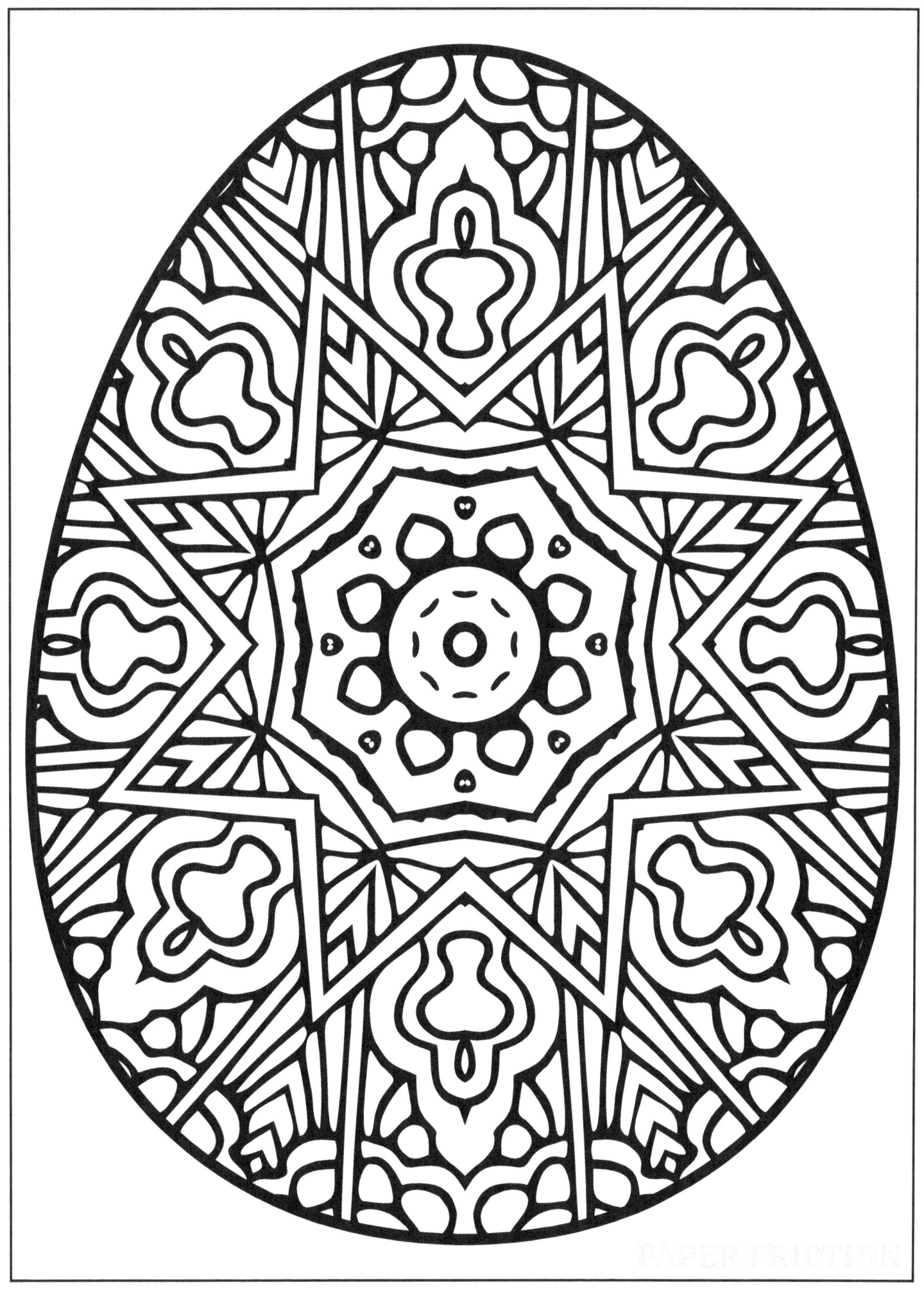

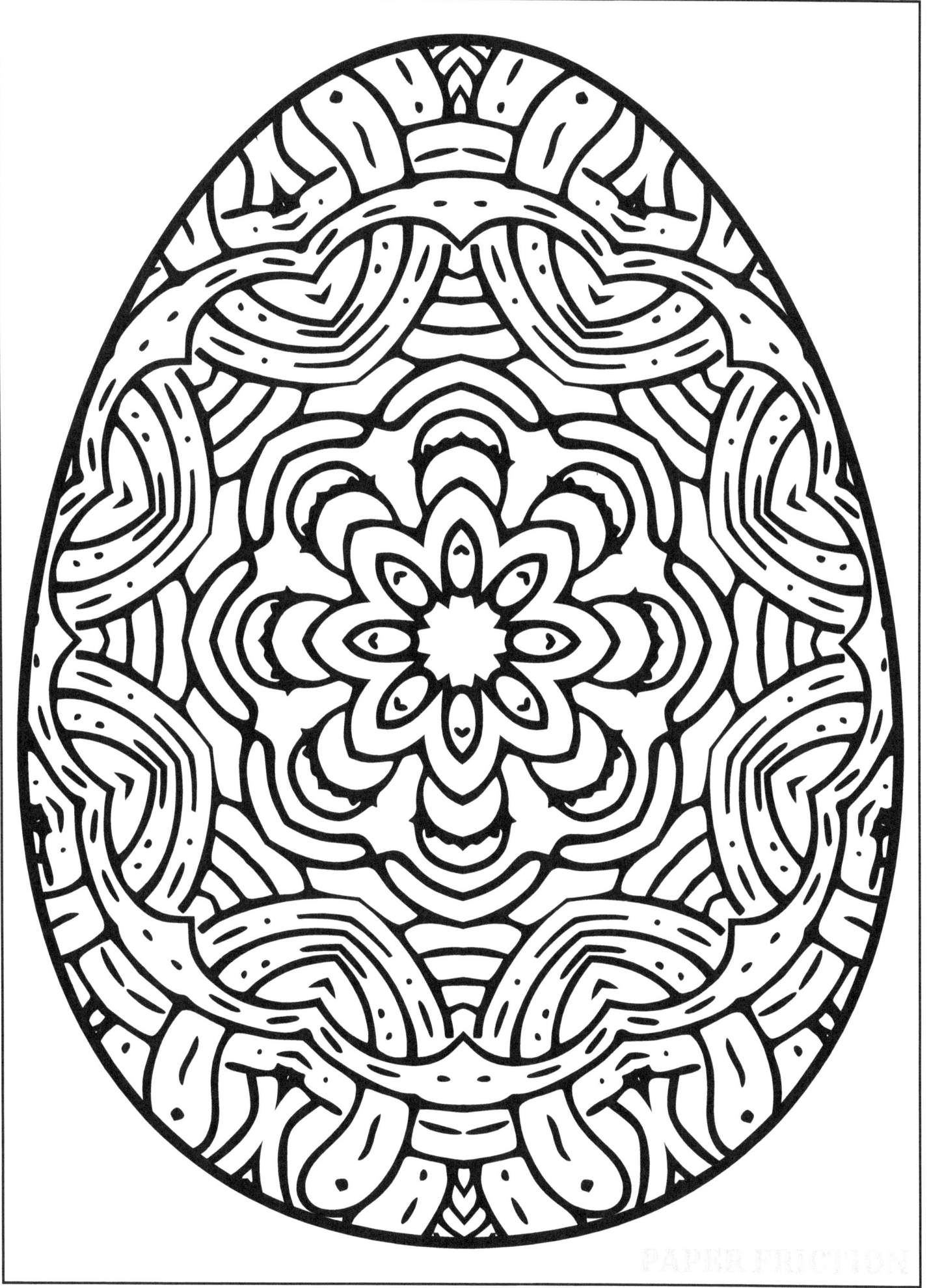